SCOTT FORESMAN

Envision It! | Handbook

D1276972

Reading STREET

Grade 4

PEARSON

Glenview, Illinois
Boston, Massachusetts
Chandler, Arizona
Upper Saddle River, New Jersey

ISBN-13: 978-0-328-60716-7
ISBN-10:   0-328-60716-9
4 5 6 7 8 9 10 V042 18 17 16 15 14 13 12 11 10

Envision It! | TEKS Handbook

Contents

Comprehension Strategies

Comprehension strategies are ways to think about reading in order to better understand what you read.

As you read,
- focus on the text.
- try to make sense of what you are reading.
- notice when you don't understand something.
- figure out how to understand the confusing parts.

Ready to Try It?

Envision It! | Visual Strategies

Background Knowledge

Important Ideas

Inferring

Monitor and Clarify

Predict and Set Purpose

Questioning

Story Structure

Summarize

Text Structure

Visualize

Background Knowledge

Background knowledge is what you already know about a topic based on your reading and personal experience. Make connections to people, places, and things. Use background knowledge before, during, and after reading to monitor comprehension.

To use background knowledge

- with fiction, preview the title, author's name, and illustrations
- with nonfiction, preview chapter titles, headings, graphics, and other text features
- think about what you already know

Officer Lee and Freckles remind me of characters in a fantastic book I am reading about working dogs.

Let's Think About Reading!

When I use background knowledge, I ask myself

- Does this character remind me of someone?
- How is this story or text similar to others I have read?
- What else do I know about this topic from what I've read or seen?

Background Knowledge
What Jo Did
by Charles R. Smith Jr.

When we use our background knowledge to help us understand what we read, we try to connect it to what we already know.

We think about what we know:

 from our own life (Text to Self)

 from the world around us (Text to World)

 from other things we've read (Text to Text)

Here are some connections I made while reading What Jo Did:

 = It reminds me of my softball team, which has mostly boys.

 = What Jo Did reminds me of Because of Winn-Dixie because both girls meet new friends.

= I'm a tomboy like Jo. I like to wear my hair up under a baseball cap, and I like sports.

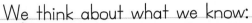 = It reminds me of the Olympic basketball games on television.

Important Ideas

Important ideas are essential ideas in a nonfiction selection. Important ideas include information that provide clues to the author's purpose.

To identify important ideas
- read all titles, headings, and captions
- look for words in italics, boldface print, or bulleted lists
- look for signal words and phrases: *for example, most important,* and others
- use any photos, illustrations, diagrams or maps
- note how the text is organized—cause and effect, problem and solution, or other ways

Wow! The lettering is in bold type.

It must be an important idea.

Types of Clouds

Let's Think About Reading!

When I identify important ideas, I ask myself
- What information is included in bold, italics or other special lettering?
- What details support important ideas?
- Are there signal words and phrases?
- What do illustrations, photos, diagrams, and charts show?
- How is the text organized?
- Why did the author write this?

Important Ideas
The Man Who Named the Clouds
by Julie Hannah and Joan Holub

These are some important ideas I learned from this biography.

- Luke Howard was interested in weather since he was a boy.
- Luke recorded weather conditions and painted pictures of different kinds of clouds.
- In 1896 an official classification of cloud names was created. All of the names were based on categories Luke had made.
- There are ten kinds of clouds.
- Cloud names refer to their shapes and how high they are.

Knowing these important ideas helped me better understand the selection. They also helped me identify the clouds that I see outside!

Inferring

When we **infer** we use background knowledge with clues in the text to come up with our own ideas about what the author is trying to present.

To infer

- identify what you already know
- combine what you know with text clues to come up with your own ideas

Let's Think About Reading!

When I infer, I ask myself
- What do I already know?
- Which text clues are important?
- What is the author trying to present?

Inferring
How Tía Lola Came to ~~Visit~~ Stay
by Julia Alvarez

Clues from Text	Inferences
Miguel finds a photograph of Colonel Charlebois as a boy with his baseball team.	He must like baseball.
The Colonel says he'd be honored to have the team practice in the pasture.	He must not be as mean as Miguel thinks he is.
Tía Lola trims the bushes into shapes of pineapples, parrots, and palm trees. Then she begins to paint the house purple.	She doesn't do things like other people do.
Tía Lola makes smoothies for the team after each practice, and she sews uniforms.	She is a hard worker.
Tía Lola names the team CHARLIE'S BOYS.	She thought the Colonel would let the family stay there if he felt part of the team.

After reading the story, I inferred that Tía Lola was a happy, loving person who believed she could change people's attitudes with her kindness and sense of fun.

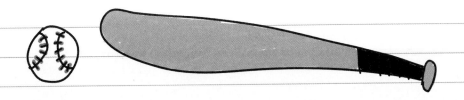

Monitor and Clarify

We **monitor comprehension** to check our understanding of what we've read. We **clarify** to find out why we haven't understood what we've read and to adjust comprehension.

To monitor and clarify

- use background knowledge as you read
- try different strategies: reread, ask questions, or use text features and illustrations

Let's Think About Reading!

When I monitor and clarify, I ask myself
- Do I understand what I'm reading?
- What doesn't make sense?
- What fix-up strategies can I use?

Monitor and Clarify
Horse Heroes
by Kate Petty

When you MONITOR, you think about what you're reading and whether or not it makes sense to you. If something doesn't make sense, you stop reading to clarify.

To CLARIFY, you reread, ask yourself questions, or read more slowly.

In Horse Heroes, I read that seeing a rickety old rope bridge made Tschiffley's blood run cold. Why would seeing a bridge scare someone so much? Then I read that the bridge stretched over a deep gorge, and that if he slipped, he might die. Now I know why Tschiffley was scared!

There are a lot of numbers and dates in the article. I made sure I read a little more slowly so that I would understand the information.

Predict and Set Purpose

We **predict** to tell what might happen next in a story or article. The prediction is based on what has already happened. We **set a purpose** to guide our reading.

To predict and set a purpose
- preview the title, author's name, and illustrations or graphics
- identify why you're reading
- use what you already know to make predictions
- look back at your predictions to confirm them

Let's Think About Reading!

When I predict and set a purpose, I ask myself
- What do I already know?
- What do I think will happen?
- What is my purpose for reading?

Predict and Set Purpose
The Seeker of Knowledge
by James Rumford

Before I read <u>Seeker of Knowledge</u>, I looked through the text and noticed lots of drawings with explanations.

Then I asked myself these questions.

Who was the seeker?

What knowledge was he seeking?

Answering those questions was my purpose for reading.

As I read, I learned that the seeker was a French boy named Jean-François Champollion. He said one day he'd be able to read Egyptian writing (hieroglyphs). I predicted that he would figure it out.

Jean-François figured out that the symbols of hieroglyphs represented syllables or whole words. That breakthrough was the key to understanding the meanings of the hieroglyphs.

My prediction was correct! Jean-François learned how to read Egyptian writing! AWESOME!

Questioning

Questioning is asking good questions about important text information. Questioning takes place before, during, and after reading.

To question
- read with a question in mind
- stop, think, and record your questions as you read
- make notes when you find information
- check your understanding and ask questions to clarify

Let's Think About Reading!

When I question, I ask myself
- Have I asked a good question with a question word?
- What questions help me make sense of my reading?
- What does the author mean?

Questioning
My Brother Martin
by Christine King Farris

As I looked through the pictures of this biography
about the Rev. Dr. Martin Luther King Jr.,
I asked myself:
> Who are all the people in the pictures?
> What was Dr. King like as a boy?
> Why does the story end with a speech?

As I read, I found answers to my questions.
> Who are all the people in the pictures?
>> The people in the pictures are family members.
> What was Dr. King like as a boy?
>> He liked playing with his brother and sister. He
didn't like piano lessons. He got into trouble sometimes.
> Why does the story end with a speech?
>> It ends with a speech because Dr. King gave a lot of
>> important speeches. He talked about wanting black
>> people to have the same rights as white people.

One question came up as I was reading that wasn't answered:
Why didn't Mother Dear explain segregation to her children
earlier?

Story Structure

Story structure is the arrangement of a story from beginning to end. You can use this information to summarize the plot.

To identify story structure
- note the conflict, or problem, at the beginning of a story
- track the rising action as conflict builds in the middle
- recognize the climax when the characters face the conflict
- identify how the conflict gets resolved and the story ends

Problem/Conflict

Rising Action

Resolution

Let's Think About Reading!

When I identify story structure, I ask myself
- What is the story's conflict or problem?
- How does the conflict build throughout the story?
- How is the conflict resolved in the end?
- How might this affect future events?

Story Structure
The Horned Toad Prince
by Jackie Mims Hopkins

Story structure is the way an author arranges the events of a story.

1. Conflict (or problem)
2. Rising Action (building conflict)
3. Climax (facing conflict)
4. Resolution (problem solved)

In The Horned Toad Prince, the story's events are set up like this:

1. Conflict: A great gust of wind blows off the hat of a cowgirl, Reba Jo. It falls into a well.

2. Rising action: A horned toad tells Reba Jo that he will get her hat if she does three favors for him. She leaves without doing the favors, and the toad follows her home and asks again.

3. Climax: The toad tells Reba Jo that he'll leave if she kisses him. She kisses the toad, and the toad turns into a prince!

4. Resolution: The prince tells Reba Jo that the great spirit of the arroyo put a spell on him and turned him into a horned toad. Reba Jo's kiss broke the spell and turned him back into a prince!

Summarize

We **summarize**, or retell, to check our understanding of what we've read. A summary is a brief statement—no more than a few sentences—and maintains a logical order.

To summarize fiction
- tell what happens in the story
- include the goals of the characters, how they try to reach them, and whether or not they succeed

To summarize nonfiction
- tell the main idea
- think about text structure and how the selection is organized

I swerved, and the squirrel ran off into the bushes!

You nearly hit a squirrel!

Let's Think About Reading!

When I summarize, I ask myself
- What is the story or selection mainly about?
- In fiction, what are the characters' goals? Are they successful?
- In nonfiction, how is the information organized?

Summarize
Because of Winn-Dixie
by Kate DiCamillo

When I summarize a story, I think of what happens in the beginning, in the middle, and at the end. Then I think about how to retell what happened in a few sentences in my own words.

This is my summary of Because of Winn-Dixie.

Opal is a new girl in town. She visits the town library, and her dog scares the librarian, Miss Franny Block. Miss Franny thinks the dog is a bear. Once Opal calms Miss Franny down, Miss Franny tells Opal about the day a bear really did visit the library. That's how Opal, Miss Franny, and a dog named Winn-Dixie all become friends.

(By the way, this is a REALLY good book! You should read it!)

21

Text Structure

We use **text structure** to look for the way the author has organized the text; for example, cause and effect, problem and solution, sequence, or compare and contrast. Analyze text structure before, during, and after reading to locate information.

To identify text structure
- before reading: preview titles, headings, and illustrations
- during reading: notice the organization
- after reading: recall the organization and summarize the text

The Youth Baseball Guide uses compare and contrast organization as its text structure.

Let's Think About Reading!

When I identify text structure, I ask myself
- What clues do titles, headings, and illustrations provide?
- How is information organized?
- How does the organization help my understanding?

Text Structure
Antarctic Journal
by Jennifer Owings Dewey

Text structure is the way nonfiction is organized.

Antarctic Journal is a journal. I previewed the journal and I noticed that it's organized like a diary or a log. The overall text structure of this journal is time order, or sequence. Each entry has a date. Within most of the journal entries there is a text structure of sequence too.

Some entries are organized differently, though. The December 24th entry has a cause-and-effect structure. When the author took a walk on the glacier, warming weather caused a crevasse (CAUSE). The author fell into it (EFFECT). Then, because of the growing cracks in the glacier (CAUSE), the author had to crawl down the glacier to safety (EFFECT).

The main text structure of sequence made me feel like I was there learning about Antarctica with the author. I looked forward to what would happen each day!!!

Visualize

We **visualize** to create a picture or pictures in our mind as we read. This helps us monitor our comprehension.

To visualize

- combine what you already know with details from the text to make pictures in your mind
- use all your senses to put yourself in the story or text

TODAY:

Pineapple pizza with cheese: spicy sauce and sweet pineapple sprinkled on top

Let's Think About Reading!

When I visualize, I ask myself
- What do I already know?
- Which details create pictures in my mind?
- How can my senses put me in the story?

Visualize
The Case of the Gasping Garbage
by Michele Torrey

When I read, I use details in a story to create a picture in my mind of what I am reading. I also use all of my senses to put myself in the text.

Many details describe the gasping garbage can in The Case of the Gasping Garbage. I can picture in my mind the can rocking back and forth. I can hear the gasping, burping, and belching sounds coming from the can. Other details help me understand how it feels (light) and how it smells (like bread). These details put me in the story. Like Drake, I wouldn't take the lid off either!

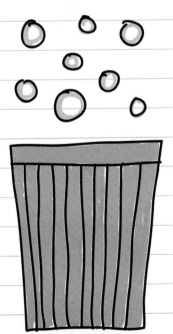

Using sensory details from the story, I can also visualize the two detectives. Drake has wild cinnamon-colored hair that sticks straight up. He wears his round glasses perched on the end of his nose. Nell, Drake's partner, has a coffee-colored ponytail and a grim smile. I can hear their surgical gloves snap into place as they begin their investigation.

Comprehension Skills

Comprehension skills are routines that you use automatically in order to better understand what you read.

As you read:
- pay attention to the way in which the text is organized.
- compare what you are reading with other things you have read.
- know what you need to look for and the ways in which to find it.
- consider the reasons why the author wrote the story or text.

Ready to Try It?

Envision It! | Visual Skills

Author's Purpose

Cause and Effect

Compare and Contrast

Draw Conclusions

Fact and Opinion

Generalize

Graphic Sources

Literary Elements

Main Idea and Details

Sequence

Classify and Categorize

Author's Purpose

Inform

Entertain

An author writes for many purposes, some of which are to inform, entertain, persuade, or express a mood or feeling. An author may have more than one purpose for writing. Sometimes the author's purpose is directly stated, but other times you have to figure it out on your own.

Persuade

Express

How to Find Author's Purpose

Is the author writing to persuade, to inform, to entertain, or to express ideas and feelings?

See It!

- Before you read, look at the images. What do you see? How do the images make you feel? Why do you think those images were chosen?

- Are there a lot of subheads, text boxes, or other graphics in the selection? Why might those features be used in this text?

- Is the text bright and colorful? What about the size and shape of the words? What kind of punctuation do you notice? Does this give you an idea about the author's purpose?

Say It!

- Take turns reading aloud and listening to the first paragraph of the text with a partner.

- Discuss: What kinds of words does the author use? Do the words make it sound like he or she is trying to persuade you? What about entertain or inform? Express ideas?

- Imagine how the author's voice might sound as you read, or your partner reads aloud. Would he or she speak with a serious tone, or one more lighthearted? Why do you think so?

Do It!

- Write the author's main ideas in your own words. Examine what you wrote. What is the author trying to show?

- Make a graphic organizer like the one below.

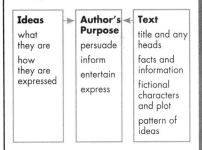

- Pretend you are the author of the text, giving a "book talk." What would you say and why? Write and rehearse a short skit with a partner.

TEKS
RC-4.C.1 Monitor comprehension.
RC-4.C.2 Adjust comprehension.

Envision It! | Skill Strategy

Skill

Strategy

Comprehension Skill

Author's Purpose

• The author's purpose is the reason or reasons an author has for writing.

• An author may write to persuade, to inform, to entertain, or to express ideas and feelings.

• Use the graphic organizer below to identify author's purpose as you read "Jefferson's Bargain."

	Author's Purpose	Why do you think so?
Before you read: What do you think it will be?		
As you read: What do you think it is?		

Comprehension Strategy

Questioning

As you read, ask questions. Think of a question before you read and make notes as you find the answer. When you ask a literal question, the answer can be found in the text. An interpretive question is answered by using other information in the text to figure out an answer on your own. An evaluative question is answered by making a judgment. You will go beyond the text to answer the question.

Jefferson's BARGAIN

About 200 years ago, when the United States was still new, our third President, Thomas Jefferson, had a big idea. He wanted to discover what lay west of the Mississippi River. This land was known as Louisiana.

Today one of our southern states is called Louisiana. But at that time, "Louisiana" was all of the land between the Mississippi River in the east and the Rocky Mountains in the west. This was an area of more than 800,000 square miles!

France said it owned this land. However, it was at war with England. It didn't want to fight another war with the United States over Louisiana. So France agreed to sell the land. President Jefferson got it for—are you ready?—less than 3 cents an acre!

The land became known as the Louisiana Purchase. In time it would become all or part of thirteen states. But when Jefferson sent Lewis and Clark to explore this area in May of 1804, the two men and their group would enter a far-reaching wilderness.

Skill Look at the title and skim the text. Why do you think the author wrote this article?

Strategy Ask questions as you read. Is the area of Louisiana 800,000 square miles today?

Strategy •Ask a literal question about what you have read.
•Ask a question that can be answered by interpreting what you have read.
•Ask evaluative questions about what you have read.

Your Turn!

❚❚ Need a Review? See the *Envision It!* Skills and Strategies for additional help.

▶ Ready to Try It? As you read other text, use what you've learned about author's purpose and questioning to help you understand it.

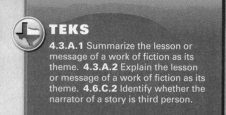

TEKS

4.3.A.1 Summarize the lesson or message of a work of fiction as its theme. **4.3.A.2** Explain the lesson or message of a work of fiction as its theme. **4.6.C.2** Identify whether the narrator of a story is third person.

Envision It! | **Skill Strategy**

Skill

Strategy

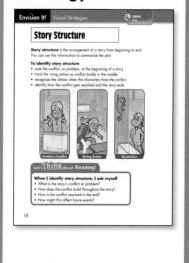

READING STREET ONLINE
ENVISION IT! ANIMATIONS
www.TexasReadingStreet.com

Comprehension Skill

🎯 Author's Purpose

- An author may write to persuade, inform, entertain, or express ideas or feelings.

- An author can have more than one purpose. The theme of a story can teach a moral or lesson as well as entertain.

- Use this chart to identify the author's purpose as you read "The Fox and the Grapes."

Ideas	Author's Purpose	Text
what they are how they are expressed	→ persuade inform entertain express ←	title and any heads facts and information fictional characters and plot pattern of ideas

Comprehension Strategy

🎯 Story Structure

Readers note the structure of fiction: the problem or goal, rising action (building up to the climax), climax (where the conflict is confronted), and outcome (where the conflict is resolved). Readers also know when a story is told by a character involved in the action (first person) or by one not involved in the action (third person).

The Fox and the Grapes

Adapted from Aesop

There once was a hungry fox who came upon a grapevine wound around a high trellis. Hanging from the vine was a bunch of grapes.

"What DEE-LISH-US looking grapes," the fox said to himself. "I think I'll just step up and grab a few." So he stood up on his hind legs under the trellis, but the grapes were out of reach.

"Hmmm," said the fox. "Those DEE-licious grapes are higher up than I thought." So the fox jumped up as high as he could, but the grapes were still out of reach.

"This is ridiculous," said the fox. "How hard can it be to grab some dee-licious grapes?" So the fox stepped back, took a running leap—and missed. The grapes were still out of reach.

"Humph!" said the fox, walking away with a toss of his tail. "I thought at first those grapes looked delicious, but now I see they are sour."

Skill What do you think the author's purpose will be? Look at the title, the byline, and the illustrations for clues.

Strategy What is the rising action, the climax, and the resolution of the story? Who is describing the action?

Skill Summarize the lesson about life this Aesop fable teaches us. Explain the message it gives the reader.

Your Turn!

⏸ **Need a Review?** See the *Envision It!* Skills and Strategies for additional help.

▶ **Ready to Try It?** As you read other text, use what you've learned about author's purpose and story structure to help you understand it.

TEKS

4.11.A.1 Summarize the main idea in text in ways that maintain meaning. **4.11.A.2** Summarize the supporting details in text in ways that maintain meaning. **Also RC-4.A.2.**

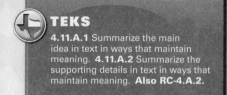

Envision It! | Skill Strategy

Skill

Strategy

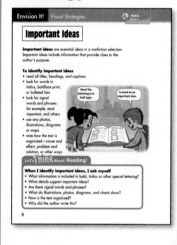

READING STREET ONLINE ENVISION IT! ANIMATIONS
www.TexasReadingStreet.com

Comprehension Skill

Author's Purpose

- Four common reasons authors have for writing are to persuade, to inform, to express ideas or feelings, or to entertain.

- Authors often have more than one purpose for writing. An author may write to both inform and entertain.

- When you figure out an author's purpose, you can adjust the way you read. You might read a funny story faster than a news article.

- Use the graphic organizer to identify author's purpose as you read "Parachutes All over the World."

Ideas	**Genre**	**Author's Purpose**
What are they? How are they expressed?	Nonfiction? Fiction?	Persuade? Inform? Entertain? Express?

Comprehension Strategy

Important Ideas

Good readers try to identify the important, or main, ideas presented in a selection to help them determine an author's purpose for writing. The important or main ideas can help you understand the topic of a selection. Details in the text can support the important ideas, but you need to know the difference between important ideas and interesting ideas.

Parachutes
All over the World

One of the first pictures of a parachute was drawn by Leonardo da Vinci in 1480! Da Vinci was a gifted Italian artist. People wonder how he ever thought of a parachute in the first place, because it was about four hundred years before the Wright brothers flew their plane at Kitty Hawk.

A French scientist, Louis-Sébastien Lenormand, who lived in the 1700s, is thought to have been the first person to use a parachute successfully. He named the parachute using the French words *parasol* (sun shield) and *chute* (fall). Lenormand tested it by jumping out of a very tall tree.

Many have contributed to the modern parachute. In San Francisco in 1885, Thomas Scott Baldwin became the first American to fall from a hot-air balloon with a parachute. In 1911, Gleb Kotelnikov, a Russian, had the idea of putting a parachute inside a knapsack. Before that, parachutes were held close to the body with both hands, very tightly.

Skill Look at the title, photograph, and diagram. What do you think is the author's purpose for writing the article?

Strategy Summarize two important or main ideas the author wants you to know about the role Lenormand played in the development of the parachute.

Strategy Summarize the most important idea of this paragraph. Summarize the details supporting it.

Your Turn!

 Need a Review? See the *Envision It!* Skills and Strategies for additional help.

▶ **Ready to Try It?** Use what you've learned about author's purpose and important ideas as you read other text.

Cause and Effect

How to Identify Cause and Effect

A cause tells why something happened. An effect is what happened.

See It!

- Look for clue words in a text, such as *because, so, since,* and *for that reason.* They can tell about cause and effect.

- Make a picture in your mind as you read the following: *Nicole spilled a glass of water on the floor. Jeff walked into the room and slipped.* Identify the cause by answering, "What happened first?" Identify the effect by answering, "What happened afterward?"

- Search for clues in illustrations that tell you about what happened and why.

Say It!

- To understand cause and effect, stop during or after reading to ask yourself, "What happened?" and "Why did this happen?"

- Take turns telling a partner what happened in a story, and how it happened.

- Listen to a partner read sentences or paragraphs aloud. Try to hear clue words, such as *because* or *so,* that tell about cause and effect.

Do It!

- Write an effect to the following cause: *The temperature dropped to 40 degrees Fahrenheit when we were outside.*

- Make a graphic organizer like the one below.

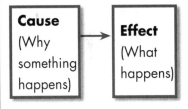

- Write "what" and "why" questions about what you have read to a partner. Have your partner answer aloud or in writing.

TEKS

RC-4.C.1 Monitor comprehension.
RC-4.C.2 Adjust comprehension.
4.11.C.1 Describe explicit relationships
among ideas in texts organized by
cause-and-effect. **Also 4.11.C.4.**

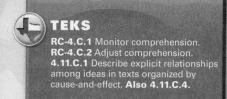

Envision It! | Skill Strategy

Skill

Strategy

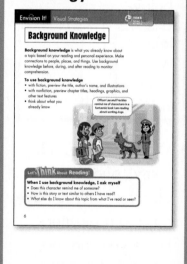

READING STREET ONLINE
ENVISION IT! ANIMATIONS
www.TexasReadingStreet.com

Comprehension Skill

Cause and Effect

- The *cause* is why something happened. The *effect* is what happened.

- Clue words such as *because, so,* and *cause* sometimes signal an explicit cause-and-effect relationship. For example, *It started to snow so the girl put on her hat.* This sentence shows an explicit relationship between a cause and an effect.

- Sometimes there are no clue words. The relationship is implicit. You have to figure out for yourself that one thing causes another.

- A cause can have more than one effect.

- Use the graphic organizer to identify causes and their effects as you read "Up, Up, and Down."

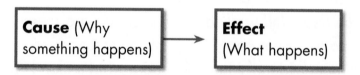

Comprehension Strategy

Background Knowledge

Good readers use their background knowledge to help them understand what they read. As you read new information, think about whether you have ever seen or experienced what you are reading about.

Up, Up, and Down

Did you ever see basketball players leap high into the air to shoot a ball into a basket? Or even higher still to block a shot? How do they jump so high?

The trick is to beat Earth's gravity. Because of this force, a person is pulled to the ground. To move away from this force, you need energy.

Think of a spring, or better yet, think of a spring in a pogo stick. Your weight on the stick presses the spring down. That stores energy in the spring. When that energy is released, it is enough to lift the stick and you off the ground.

In a similar way, you can build up energy in your legs. If you stand straight and then try to jump up, you can't. You may be able to lift off the ground an inch or so, but that's all. That's why you bend at the knees before jumping up. When you bend, it's as if you are putting a "spring" in your legs. Release that spring, and up you go.

Of course, the energy is not nearly enough to overcome Earth's gravity. That's why Earth will always pull you back down again.

Skill Look for a clue word in this paragraph to help find the cause-and-effect relationship. Is the relationship explicit or implicit?

Skill Look for causes and their effects in this paragraph. What causes energy to be stored? What effect does releasing it have?

Strategy Think of what you know about jumping off the ground as you read this paragraph. Explain what that "spring" feels like.

Your Turn!

 Need a Review? See the *Envision It!* Skills and Strategies for additional help.

▶ **Ready to Try It?** Use what you've learned about cause and effect and background knowledge as you read other text.

TEKS

RC-4.A.1 Establish purposes for reading selected texts based upon own desired outcome to enhance comprehension. **Also 4.11.C.1, 4.11.C.4.**

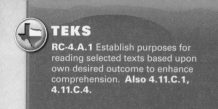

Envision It! Skill Strategy

Skill

Strategy

Comprehension Skill

Cause and Effect

- A cause is *why* something happens. An effect is *what* happens.

- Clue words such as *because, so,* and *cause* sometimes signal an explicit cause-and-effect relationship. Where there are no clue words, the relationship is implicit and you must figure out for yourself that one thing causes another.

- A cause can have more than one effect.

- Use the graphic organizer to identify causes and their effects as you read "Name That Hurricane."

Comprehension Strategy

Predict and Set Purpose

Before you read, look over an article to predict what it is about. Predicting helps you set a purpose for reading, such as to be entertained or to be informed. Setting a purpose helps you determine how you should read the text. It will also help you understand what you read.

NAME THAT HURRICANE

A hurricane is a huge storm with powerful winds that form over the ocean. Sometimes, these storms hit land. Weather scientists, or meteorologists, track these storms to warn people. There can be more than one storm going on at a time, so to communicate without confusion, meteorologists give each storm a name.

Hurricane names are taken from a list on a six-year cycle. In other words, every six years the same names are used, but not all the names are needed every year. It depends on the number of hurricanes that year. The first storm of each season has a name that starts with the letter A, and they follow alphabetically after that. A few letters in the alphabet don't begin many common names, so these are not used in the naming line up—Q, U, X, Y, and Z.

Some hurricanes have been so destructive that their names have been "retired," and will never be used again. For example, there will never be another Hurricane Andrew. This monster storm slammed into the Bahamas, Florida, and Louisiana in 1992, killing 54 people and causing billions of dollars in damage.

Strategy Look over the article before you begin reading. Predict what the article will be about. Set your purpose for reading.

Skill What causes meteorologists to name hurricanes? Is this information an explicitly stated relationship or is it an implicit relationship?

Skill What causes some hurricane names to be "retired"? Is this cause-and-effect relationship explicit or implicit?

Your Turn!

 Need a Review? See the *Envision It!* Skills and Strategies for additional help.

▶ **Ready to Try It?** As you read other text, look for cause-and-effect relationships and predict and set purposes to help you understand it.

TEKS

4.11.C.1 Describe explicit relationships among ideas in texts organized by cause-and-effect. **RC-4.B.1** Ask literal questions of text. **RC-4.B.2** Ask interpretive questions of text. **RC-4.B.3** Ask evaluative questions of text.

Envision It! | Skill Strategy

Skill

Strategy

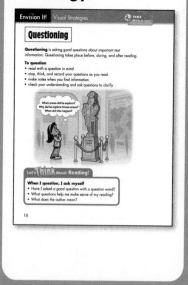

READING STREET ONLINE
ENVISION IT! ANIMATIONS
www.TexasReadingStreet.com

Comprehension Skill

Cause and Effect

- The *effect* is what happens. The *cause* is why it happens.

- Clue words such as *because, so, therefore,* and *as a result* signal explicit causes and effects. When there aren't any clue words, the relationship will be implicit. You will have to figure out the relationship for yourself.

- Sometimes one effect becomes the cause of another effect, which causes another, and so on. This is called a chain of events.

- Use the graphic organizer to identify the chain of events Rosa Parks set in motion as you read "Rosa Parks Started Something Big."

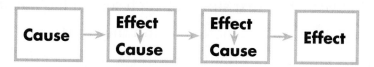

Comprehension Strategy

Questioning

Good readers ask different types of questions as they read. When you ask a literal question, the answer can be found "right there" in the text. An interpretive question is answered by using other information in the text to figure out an answer on your own. An evaluative question is answered by making a judgment. You will go beyond the text to answer the question.

Rosa Parks
Started Something Big

Rosa Parks was tired. She had worked hard all day. To ride home, she took a seat on the Cleveland Avenue bus in Montgomery, Alabama.

On that evening of December 1, 1955, segregation was the law. That meant white people could ride in the front of the bus, but black people had to ride in the back. Black people could sit in the middle rows—as long as no white people wanted those seats.

Rosa Parks, an African American, was settled in the first row of the section for black people when a white man demanded her seat. She refused to get up.

Because she refused, the bus driver called the police. Rosa Parks was arrested. Black people throughout the city protested by refusing to ride the buses. This action, called a boycott, was organized by a minister named Martin Luther King Jr. After more than a year, the law was changed. Segregation on buses was no longer allowed.

Because of Martin Luther King Jr.'s work, he became widely known. He went on to lead the struggle for African Americans' rights throughout the country.

Skill What effect did the law regarding segregation on buses have on black people in Montgomery, Alabama, in 1955?

Skill What was the final effect in the chain of events that started with Rosa's action?

Strategy •Ask a literal question about what you have read. •Ask a question that can be answered by interpreting what you have read. •Ask a question that can be answered by making a judgment about what you have read.

Your Turn!

 Need a Review? See the *Envision It!* Skills and Strategies for additional help.

Ready to Try It? Use what you've learned about cause and effect and questioning as you read other text.

Compare and Contrast

To compare and contrast is to look for similarities and differences in things.

How to Compare and Contrast

When we compare things, we say what is similar about them.
When we contrast things, we say what is different about them.

See It!

- Look at page 44. What does it tell you about comparing and contrasting?

- Look at the illustrations that go with a story you are reading. If characters are pictured, compare and contrast them. You might notice that certain characters have the same or different posture, facial expression, body type, hair, or eye color.

- Look for words such as *like, as,* and *same* that signal two things are similar. Look for words such as *but, unlike,* and *different* to show differences.

Say It!

- Tell a partner how you are alike and different from a family member. For example: *My brother is loud and talkative, but I am shy and quiet. However, we both like to play baseball.*

- As you read, stop at parts of the story that might describe things that are similar or different. Explain these similarities or differences to a partner.

- Name an item in the classroom. Have a partner tell you one thing in the classroom that is similar to that object, and one thing that is different.

Do It!

- A Venn diagram is helpful when you want to tell how things are alike or different. However, it's not the only kind of graphic organizer you can use to make comparisons. Try this one, below:

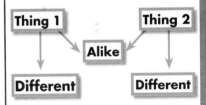

- With your teacher, gather small items around the classroom that you can easily compare and contrast. How are the things you've chosen alike? How are they different?

45

TEKS
4.3.B.1 Compare the adventures or exploits of characters in traditional and classical literature. **4.3.B.2** Contrast the adventures or exploits of characters in traditional and classical literature. **Also RC-4.C.1, RC-4.C.2.**

Envision It! | Skill Strategy

Skill

Strategy

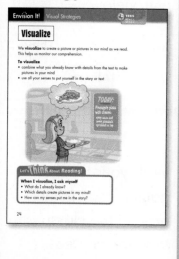

READING STREET ONLINE
ENVISION IT! ANIMATIONS
www.TexasReadingStreet.com

Comprehension Skill

Compare and Contrast

- When you compare and contrast, you tell how two or more things are alike and different.

- You can compare and contrast two or more things you read about or compare something you read about with something you already know.

- Use the graphic organizer below to compare and contrast Encyclopedia Brown and Nancy Drew as you read "Detective Techniques."

	Alike	Different
Two things in the text		
One thing in the text with something I already know		

Comprehension Strategy

Visualize

Good readers visualize as they read. Visualizing helps readers form mental pictures of what they are reading to help them understand ideas and information. Try to picture in your mind what the author has written to help the story come to life.

Detective Techniques

Kim and Tomas were talking about books they liked to read. "I really enjoy a good, suspenseful, detective mystery story," Kim said.

"Me too!" said Tomas. "Who's your favorite?"

"I think Encyclopedia Brown is great," Kim said. "I love when he closes his eyes and pieces the clues together."

"Really? I get bored when he does that," Tomas answered. "I like the way he listens to all the facts about a crime, and then tells about all the ways it might have been committed. Sometimes he's got the mystery figured out before he goes to the crime scene!"

"Then there's Nancy Drew," said Kim. "She really jumps right in and starts snooping around. She's always exploring the crime scene—going into spooky old houses and deserted castles searching for a clue. I get the shivers when the story gets dark and creepy—but I still have to keep reading!"

"That's what I love about mysteries!" Tomas said. "That suspenseful feeling—knowing *something* is going to happen, but you don't know what."

"Me too," Kim said. "But I *really* look forward to the end when the mystery is solved and the detective lets us know what clues led to solving the crime."

Skill Contrast Kim's and Tomas's reactions to Encyclopedia Brown. How are their reactions different?

Strategy If you visualize the spooky houses and empty castles, you will understand the suspenseful feeling Kim experiences.

Skill Compare what both Kim and Tomas love about mysteries. How are they the same?

Your Turn!

 Need a Review? See the *Envision It!* Skills and Strategies for additional help.

▶ **Ready to Try It?** As you read other text, use what you've learned about comparing and contrasting and visualizing to understand it.

TEKS

4.11.C.3 Describe explicit relationships among ideas in texts organized by comparison.
4.11.C.6 Describe implicit relationships among ideas in texts organized by comparison.
Also RC-4.E.1, RC-4.E.2.

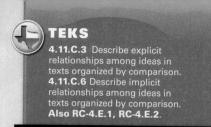

Skill

Strategy

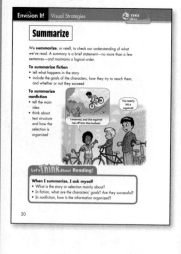

READING STREET ONLINE
ENVISION IT! ANIMATIONS
www.TexasReadingStreet.com

Comprehension Skill

Compare and Contrast

- To compare and contrast is to tell how two or more things are alike and different. These relationships may be explicit or implicit.

- Clue words such as *like* and *as* show explicitly how two things are alike. Clue words such as *but, instead,* and *unlike* show explicitly how they are different.

- Implicit comparisons don't use clue words. The reader has to figure out for him- or herself that two or more things are alike or different.

- Use this graphic organizer and what you know about explicit and implicit comparisons as you read "It's a Jungle Out There."

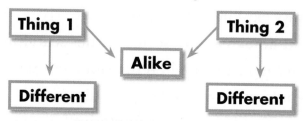

Comprehension Strategy

Summarize

Good readers summarize information in texts, while maintaining meaning. As you read, decide which are the main ideas and important details. Then put these important ideas together into a short statement, or summary. As you summarize information, keep your important ideas in logical order.

IT'S A JUNGLE OUT THERE!

Well, actually, it's a tropical rain forest out there. It's easy to confuse the terms *rain forest* and *jungle,* but they don't mean exactly the same thing. A jungle is a particular part of the rain forest.

In the rain forest, thousands and thousands of huge trees grow so close together that the tops overlap to form a kind of roof high above the forest floor. This leafy roof is called the canopy.

Strategy Summarize how the canopy in a rain forest is formed.

You can walk around fairly well on the forest floor under the canopy. That's because the tops of the tall trees grow so thickly together that they shut out most of the sunlight. Plants need sunlight to grow, but there's not enough light for them to grow under the canopy.

The jungle is another matter. In the rain forest there are clearings (for example, on the banks of rivers) where there are not as many gigantic trees. Here the sunlight can reach the ground, so smaller trees and plants can grow. And do they ever! This wild, thick tangle of plants is the jungle. You would need a big, sharp knife called a machete to hack your way through it. Good luck!

Skill The topic is shifting to the jungle. Pay attention to how it is both like and unlike the rain forest.

Skill Ask yourself how the jungle is different from the rain forest.

Need a Review? See the *Envision It!* Skill and Strategies for additional help.

Ready to Try It? As you read other text, use what you've learned about comparing and contrasting and summarizing to understand it.

TEKS

RC-4.C.1 Monitor comprehension. **RC-4.C.2** Adjust comprehension. **4.11.C.3** Describe explicit relationships among ideas in texts organized by comparison. **Also 4.11.C.6.**

Envision It! | Skill Strategy

Skill

Strategy

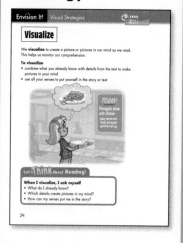

READING STREET ONLINE
ENVISION IT! ANIMATIONS
www.TexasReadingStreet.com

Comprehension Skill

Compare and Contrast

- To compare and contrast means to tell how two or more things are alike and different.

- Authors may use clue words such as *like, as,* and *same* to show explicit similarities. They may use words such as *but, unlike,* and *different* to show explicit differences.

- Authors may not use clue words when making comparisons. The reader has to figure out these implicit relationships for him- or herself.

- Use this graphic organizer to identify ideas the author compares and contrasts as you read "Archaeology: Dig It."

Similarities	Differences

Comprehension Strategy

Visualize

Active readers transform the words on the page into mental images. Visualizing similarities and differences between two people or things that are being compared helps you understand what you read.

ARCHAEOLOGY: DIG IT

Archaeology is the study of things left by people who lived in the past. Some archaeologists study people who left behind things and written records. Others study people who had no written language.

Skill What does one type of archaeologist do that the other does not? Is this an explicit or implicit comparison?

With the passing of time, ancient places often are covered with layers of earth. The archaeologist has to dig down to find the things people left behind. These things give clues to how those people lived.

Strategy What might people in the future discover about the way we live today? Visualize and describe things they might find that will tell them about us.

All people have certain things in common. We all need to eat and a place to live. So archaeologists look for things such as dishes, cooking pots, arrowheads, and hunting knives. They hope to find things people built, such as houses and roads. They study these things to understand how people lived in the past.

How we live today is different from how people lived long ago. Most of us don't hunt our food. We don't make our own cooking pots or dishes. But we do live in homes and travel on roads, and we do keep written records. We will leave behind these records for other people to read in the future.

Skill Compare and contrast the way people live today with how people lived long ago.

Your Turn!

❚❚ Need a Review? See the *Envision It!* Skills and Strategies for additional help.

▶ Ready to Try It? As you read other text, use what you've learned about comparing and contrasting and visualizing to understand it.

Draw Conclusions

When we draw conclusions, we think about facts and details and then decide something about them.

How to Draw Conclusions

When we draw conclusions, we form an opinion by combining our own background knowledge with the facts and details stated in a text.

See It!

- Look at page 52. What details do you notice? What conclusions can you make about what is happening?

- Look at the illustrations that go with your reading. How does what you see help you draw conclusions about the story? What sort of information do the images reveal?

- Picture in your mind someone who is mad, happy, sad, or excited. What kinds of clues do they give you about their mood?

Say It!

- If you feel stuck, go back and quietly read aloud places where you might find facts and details that help you draw a conclusion from what you read.

- Ask questions such as "Why is this happening?" as you read. Talk through any conclusions you make with a partner, looking back over details from the reading and what you know from your own life.

- Share with a small group what you already know about the subject you're reading about. Each group member should share what they know.

Do It!

- Make a graphic organizer like the one below to help you draw conclusions based on facts and details.

- Write a brief mystery story where the main character has to draw a conclusion based on clues. For example, the character might find out that there is a missing book in the classroom. Make sure to include facts and details that help the character solve the mystery of who took the book and why!

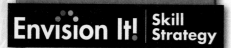

Skill

Strategy

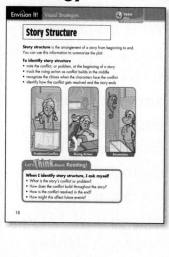

READING STREET ONLINE
ENVISION IT! ANIMATIONS
www.TexasReadingStreet.com

Comprehension Skill

Draw Conclusions

- Draw conclusions to form an opinion based on your background knowledge or on the facts and details stated in a text.

- You can draw a conclusion while you read or after you read.

- Check an author's conclusions or your own conclusions by asking: *Is this the only logical choice? Are the facts accurate?*

- Use the graphic organizer below to help you draw conclusions about the kind of dog Tumbleweed is as you read "Chasing After Tumbleweed."

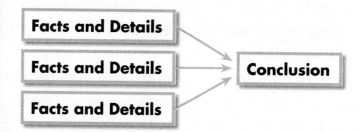

Comprehension Strategy

Story Structure

Good readers note the structure of a story they are reading in order to better understand the text. In fiction, most story events are arranged by sequence, or in time order.

CHASING AFTER TUMBLEWEED

Every morning Tumbleweed barks at the front door until we let him out to play. He loves to run all over the ranch. Some days I find him miles away at the southern border of our ranch. He knows that's where the prairie dogs hide. He loves to chase them. Getting him to come home every day is my job. It isn't an easy one!

Skill How can you use your background knowledge about dogs to draw a conclusion about Tumbleweed?

Sometimes I can convince my bus driver to stop on the way home to pick up Tumbleweed. "Make it quick!" the driver always says. "Everyone wants to get home!" That may be true. But no one seems to mind the wait as they pile to the side of the bus so they can laugh as they watch me chase Tumbleweed.

Skill Why does the bus driver stop for the narrator? Use details in the text to draw a conclusion about the bus driver.

Yesterday Dad helped me look for Tumbleweed in the helicopter. Dad uses the helicopter to drop hay to the cattle now that it's winter.

For hours we flew all over the ranch looking for Tumbleweed. But there was no sign of him. It was getting darker and colder by the minute. Where could he be?

Thankfully, my dad knows his cattle well. When he saw one cow flicking back snow with its hooves, he knew something was bothering it. He landed the helicopter and told me to go look under the cow. There he was. I'm going to have to teach Tumbleweed that it's warmer and safer underneath my bed!

Strategy Explain how the author's use of sequence helps you understand the story.

Your Turn!

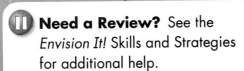

Ⅱ Need a Review? See the *Envision It!* Skills and Strategies for additional help.

 Ready to Try It?
As you read other text, use what you've learned about drawing conclusions and story structure to understand it.

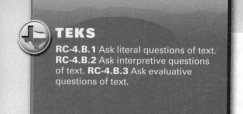
TEKS

RC-4.B.1 Ask literal questions of text.
RC-4.B.2 Ask interpretive questions of text. **RC-4.B.3** Ask evaluative questions of text.

Envision It! | Skill Strategy

Skill

Strategy

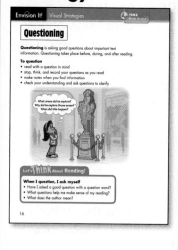

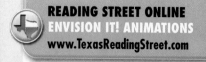
READING STREET ONLINE
ENVISION IT! ANIMATIONS
www.TexasReadingStreet.com

Comprehension Skill

Draw Conclusions

- Facts and details are the small pieces of information in an article or story.

- Facts and details "add up" to a conclusion— a decision or opinion the reader forms that makes sense.

- Use this graphic organizer to draw conclusions about why Bodie would be interesting to visit as you read "Visiting a California Ghost Town."

| Facts and Details | + | Facts and Details | = | Conclusion |

Comprehension Strategy

Questioning

Active readers ask and answer questions before, during, and after reading. When you ask a literal question, the answer can be found in the text. An interpretive question is answered by using other information in the text to figure out an answer on your own. An evaluative question is answered by making a judgment. You will go beyond the text to answer the question.

Visiting a California Ghost Town

If you have ever wondered what a real ghost town looks like, you can visit Bodie, California. A ghost town is an abandoned town that has been deserted for many years. In 1859, when gold was discovered in Bodie, the whole town had only about twenty miners. By 1880—just over twenty years later—the town's population grew to around ten thousand. A few years later, the boom was over, and by 1882 people started moving away.

In 1962, Bodie became a California State Historic Park. The park service keeps Bodie in a state of "arrested decay." This means that things are kept just as they were found many years ago. About 170 buildings are still standing and most of them are kept locked so that things inside can be kept the same as they were when the last residents left the town. If you look inside some of the buildings, it may appear that the people just left. You may even see books left open on desks or a store filled with goods.

Bodie is an incredible place to go if you like learning about the past. Walk around this town and see if you can imagine what it was like living in the Old West.

Strategy What is a "ghost town"?

Skill Why is Bodie called a ghost town?

Skill What conclusion can you draw about visiting a ghost town?

Your Turn!

⏸ **Need a Review?** See the *Envision It!* Skills and Strategies for additional help.

▶ **Ready to Try It?** As you read other text, use what you've learned about drawing conclusions and questioning to help you understand it.

TEKS
RC-4.C.1 Monitor comprehension.
RC-4.C.2 Adjust comprehension.

Envision It! | Skill Strategy

Skill

Strategy

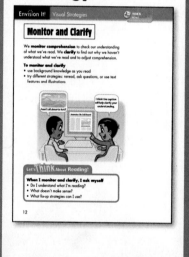

READING STREET ONLINE
ENVISION IT! ANIMATIONS
www.TexasReadingStreet.com

Comprehension Skill

🎯 Draw Conclusions

- The small pieces of information in a selection are called the facts and details.

- When you put facts and details together to form an opinion, you are drawing a conclusion. When you draw a conclusion, be sure it is supported by what you have read.

- Use the graphic organizer to draw conclusions as you read "The Man in the Moon."

Facts and Details	Facts and Details	Facts and Details

Conclusion

Comprehension Strategy

🎯 Monitor and Clarify

While you are reading, it's important to know when you don't understand something. If you are confused, stop and reread the selection aloud. Looking back and rereading is one way to clarify, or "adjust," your understanding. You might also read on to look for an explanation of what you don't understand.

The Man in the Moon

When we look up and see (with the help of our imaginations) a face in the moon, the question is not whom we see, but what we see. For when we gaze at the moon, we are seeing craters, mountains, deep narrow valleys, and wide-open plains.

The moon is a dry and airless place made up of rocks and dust. But when the telescope was first invented—about 400 years ago—people had no way of knowing that there was no water on the moon. So when they looked through the telescope and saw the open plains, they assumed they were looking at bodies of water. They named these places mares (MAH-rees), which is Latin for "seas."

Today, we know there is no water on the moon, but the names have stuck. That is why these dry and dusty places have such lovely names as Bay of Rainbows, Lake of Dreams, and Sea of Tranquillity.

Will you travel to the moon someday? Maybe. And maybe you'll come back and say, "It's a nice place to visit, but I wouldn't want to live there!"

Skill Draw a conclusion from the first sentence. Is this piece going to be science or fantasy? (It's a little tricky!)

Skill If you read these names without knowing what the moon is like, what conclusion might you draw?

Strategy Is there something about the article you don't understand? Rereading can help.

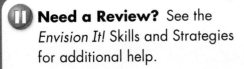

Your Turn!

Need a Review? See the *Envision It!* Skills and Strategies for additional help.

Ready to Try It? As you read other text, use what you've learned about drawing conclusions and monitoring and clarifying to help you understand it.

59

Fact and Opinion

A fact is something that can be proved true or false. An opinion can't be proved.

Fact

Wow, you blew the tuba for 45 seconds straight!

Opinion

But I think it sounds HORRIBLE!

How to Identify Fact and Opinion

A statement of fact can be proven true or false. A statement of opinion tells someone's ideas or feelings and should be supported by good logic.

See It!

- Look at page 60. What fact is being stated? What opinion is being expressed?

- Have your teacher help you look at reference books such as encyclopedias, textbooks, or credible Web sites to find out if something is true or false.

- Look for clue words that might give a hint that something is an opinion and not a fact. They include words such as *favorite, great, exciting, boring,* and other words that describe someone's beliefs or feelings.

Say It!

- With a partner, tell one fact and one opinion about something you know about. Your partner should be able to tell which is fact and which is opinion.

- Say aloud a statement of opinion to a partner, such as: *Basketball is the best sport to play.* Have your partner change your statement to one that states a fact. *(Basketball is a popular sport to play)*

- Read the following aloud, and tell which is a fact, and which is an opinion:
1. *It's freezing in here!*
2. *The thermometer says that it is 30 degrees Fahrenheit.*

Do It!

- Use a graphic organizer such as the one below to help you organize the facts and valid opinions in a text. (Note: faulty means weak or illogical.)

Statement of Fact or Opinion	How to Check Statement of Fact/ Support for Statement of Opinion	Valid or Faulty?

- Write a paragraph that tells about what you did in the morning before school. Be sure to include facts and opinions.

- Ask your teacher for permission to look at some classroom books. Record the facts and opinions you find.

TEKS

RC-4.C.1 Monitor comprehension.
RC-4.C.2 Adjust comprehension.
4.11.B.1 Distinguish fact in a text.
4.11.B.2 Distinguish opinion in a
text. **4.11.B.3** Explain how to verify
what is a fact.

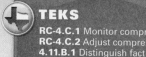

Envision It! Skill Strategy

Skill

Strategy

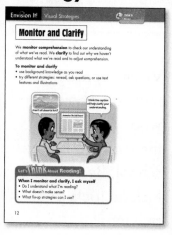

READING STREET ONLINE
ENVISION IT! ANIMATIONS
www.TexasReadingStreet.com

Comprehension Skill

Fact and Opinion

- A statement of fact can be proved true or false.

- A statement of opinion cannot be proved true or false. It is a belief or judgment.

- Use the graphic organizer to distinguish facts and opinions as you read "Bug Boys."

Statement	Fact? How Can It Be Checked?	Opinion? What Are Clue Words?

Comprehension Strategy

Monitor and Clarify

While you read, it's important to know when you understand something and when you don't. If you are confused, stop and reread the section aloud. Looking back and rereading is one way to clarify, or "adjust," your understanding of what you are reading.

Bug * Boys

In the sport of horse racing, a jockey is the one who rides the horses. Jockeys start out when they are young. An apprentice jockey is called a "bug boy" because a mark called an asterisk appears after his name in the race program. Some people think that the mark looks like a bug!

Willie Shoemaker was one of the most well-known jockeys in racing. He won his first horse race at the age of seventeen. He was small in size, weighing under one hundred pounds. Many people believe he was the greatest jockey of all time. He won the Kentucky Derby four times. Another jockey, Pat Day, started out as a rodeo cowboy. Because he was 4 feet 11 inches tall, people thought he would do well as a jockey. In 1989, he set a record when he won eight of nine races in a single day!

Chris McCarron was called the best jockey of the year in 1974. After a career as a jockey, Chris McCarron worked on the 2003 film *Seabiscuit*. The movie was about a real race.

Skill What three facts did you learn about jockeys? How can they be checked?

Skill What opinion did people have about Willie Shoemaker?

Strategy Why would his height make him a good jockey? Reread the selection for details to help understand this.

Your Turn!

 Need a Review? See the *Envision It!* Skills and Strategies for additional help.

▶ **Ready to Try It?** Use what you've learned about fact and opinion and monitoring and clarifying as you read other text.

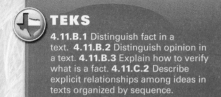

TEKS

4.11.B.1 Distinguish fact in a text. **4.11.B.2** Distinguish opinion in a text. **4.11.B.3** Explain how to verify what is a fact. **4.11.C.2** Describe explicit relationships among ideas in texts organized by sequence.

Envision It! Skill Strategy

Skill

Strategy

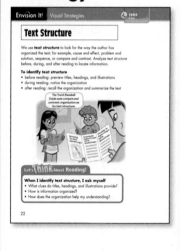

READING STREET ONLINE
ENVISION IT! ANIMATIONS
www.TexasReadingStreet.com

Comprehension Skill

Fact and Opinion

- A statement of fact can be correct or incorrect. You can check a fact by doing research.

- A statement of opinion should be supported. A valid opinion is supported by facts or good logic. A faulty opinion is not supported.

- Some sentences contain both statements of fact and statements of opinion.

- Use this graphic organizer to identify facts and opinions, and whether the opinions are valid, in "Something Must Be Done."

Statement	Support	True or False/ Valid or Faulty
Statement of fact	Other facts	True
Statement of opinion	Logic or known facts	Valid
Statement of opinion	Weak opinion or incorrect facts	Faulty

Comprehension Strategy

Text Structure

Use the text structure to help understand what you read. A nonfiction article may put events in sequence. An explicitly stated sequence uses clue words such as *first* or *next*. Or the sequence may be implicit, and the reader has to figure out the order of what happens. When you preview a text, look for features such as titles, headings, bold print, and photos to know what to expect.

SOMETHING MUST BE DONE

What is the largest animal that ever lived? Is it an elephant? Not even close. This animal can be as big as four elephants. Is it a dinosaur? No!

The largest animal in the world is the blue whale. This beautiful animal can grow to be one hundred feet long! You might think that an animal so enormous could survive anything. Not so.

Skill Some sentences contain both a statement of fact and a statement of opinion. Find the fact and opinion in this paragraph.

In the 1800s and early 1900s, whaling was big business. People killed whales to make things such as oil and candles. Whales were hunted almost to extinction. In time, other ways of lighting houses and workplaces were developed. People realized how the whaling business hurt the whales. Now, most countries ban whaling, but even so, many species are still endangered.

Skill How can the author support this statement?

Whales face other challenges too. They can get tangled in fishing nets and drown. (Remember, whales are mammals; they need to breathe air.) They can get sick from pollution. Sometimes, they collide with ships.

Strategy How does the order, or sequence, of events in this paragraph help you understand what you are reading? Is the sequence implicit or explicit? What about the last paragraph?

We need to find ways to protect whales. People can write letters to newspapers and to politicians to inform others that saving whales is important. We all can do something to help the whales and save their habitats. We can make a difference!

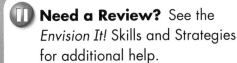

Your Turn!

 Need a Review? See the *Envision It!* Skills and Strategies for additional help.

▶ **Ready to Try It?** Use what you've learned about fact and opinion and text structure as you read other text.

TEKS

4.11.B.1 Distinguish fact in a text.
4.11.B.2 Distinguish opinion in a
text. **4.11.B.3** Explain how to verify
what is a fact. **RC-4.E.1** Summarize
information in text, maintaining
meaning. **Also 4.11.A.1, 4.11.A.2,
RC-4.E.2.**

Envision It! Skill Strategy

Skill

Strategy

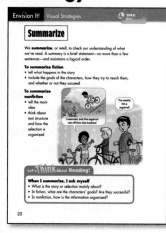

READING STREET ONLINE
ENVISION IT! ANIMATIONS
www.TexasReadingStreet.com

Comprehension Skill

🎯 Fact and Opinion

- Statements of fact can be proved true or false. Statements of opinion are judgments, beliefs, or ways of thinking about something.

- Evaluate statements of opinion by using the text, your prior knowledge, and logic. Ask: Is the statement of opinion valid? Is it supported well? Or is it faulty, without support?

- Use the graphic organizer to distinguish facts from opinions as you read "Are You Ready for Some Football?"

Statement of Fact or Opinion	How to Check Statement of Fact/ Support for Statement of Opinion	Valid or Faulty?

Comprehension Strategy

🎯 Summarize

Good readers summarize information in texts. As you read, decide what are the main ideas. Then put these ideas together in logical order into a short statement, or summary, that maintains the meaning of the text. As you summarize, does your thinking change?

ARE YOU READY FOR SOME FOOTBALL?

WHEN DID THE GAME BEGIN?

American football wasn't invented all at once. It evolved at colleges in the late 1800s from two other games: soccer and rugby. Football was like soccer in that you could move the ball toward a goal by kicking it. Football was like rugby in that you could run with the ball and tackle players.

Skill Even in this text, there can be statements of opinion. Ask: Will this statement be supported by facts or logic? Will it be valid or faulty?

PLAY NICE!

By 1900, football had become rough! A team could have as many as 25 to 30 players on the field at one time. That's a lot of people running, blocking, and tackling. Often the "game" was more like a brawl! To make matters worse, players didn't wear pads or helmets. Not a good idea! Finally, President Theodore Roosevelt said the sport must have rules for safety.

Skill Is this sentence a statement of fact or opinion? If opinion, explain if it is valid or faulty.

FOOTBALL TODAY

Over the years, the game of football has continued to change. New rules have been added, and while college football is still popular, sports fans have also grown to love professional football. In fact, do you know what the most watched American TV sports event is? The Super Bowl! It is also the best American sports event.

Strategy What is the main idea of this article? What details would you include in a summary of this article?

Your Turn!

 Need a Review? See the *Envision It!* Skills and Strategies for additional help.

▶ **Ready to Try It?** Use what you have learned about fact and opinion and summarizing as you read other text.

Generalize

To generalize is to make a broad statement or rule that applies to many examples.

How to Generalize

A generalization is a broad statement about something that can often be proved true.

See It!

- Look at the picture on page 68. What does it tell you about making generalizations?

- As you read, look for clue words that might signal a generalization, such as *many, most, usually, never, all,* or *few.*

- Look around the classroom for objects you can make a generalization about. When you have chosen an object, examine it and make a generalization about it. Remember to ask yourself if your generalization can be supported by facts.

Say It!

- Remember to look for words or phrases in your reading that make broad statements about someone or something that is often true. When you find a statement that seems to make a generalization, read it aloud to a partner. Together, talk about why this is a generalization.

- Think about people, places, or objects in your reading and ask a partner if he or she can make a generalization about them, using key words such as *all, most, many,* or *none.*

Do It!

- Use a graphic organizer such as the one below to help you make generalizations as you read. Ask yourself when making a generalization if it is supported by facts. (Note: *faulty* means unsupported, or wrong.)

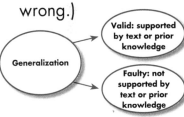

- Bring a notebook to lunch or to the playground, and look for generalizations you can make about certain foods, games, plants, and so on.

Envision It! | Skill Strategy

Skill

Strategy

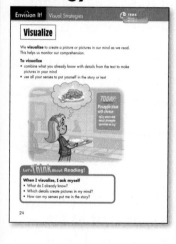

Comprehension Skill

Generalize

- A generalization is a broad statement that applies to many examples.

- Clue words, such as *all, most, always, usually,* or *generally,* signal that an author is making a generalization.

- Some generalizations are valid, which means that they are supported by facts or details. Some are faulty, which means that they are not supported.

- Use the graphic organizer to help you identify generalizations as you read "Call It a Day."

Generalization	Clue Word?

Comprehension Strategy

Visualize

Good readers visualize, or make pictures in their mind, as they read. These mental pictures can help you understand the ideas and information in the text. As you read, use the author's words to help you picture in your mind information that is unfamiliar to you.

Call It a Day

When we say *day*, we often mean daytime, when it is light out—as opposed to nighttime, when it is dark. Daytime can vary. It depends on where you are and what time of year it is. Along the equator the length of day is always the same—about 12 hours.

North or south of the equator, hours of daylight change throughout the year. In general, the farther north or south you are, the greater the change. The longest "day" of the year in the Northern Hemisphere is usually June 21. On that day, New York has about 13 hours of daylight. The North Pole has 24!

Of course, 24 hours is another meaning of day. Daytime and nighttime together make up one day. We have day and night because of the Earth's spin, or rotation.

The Earth orbits around the sun. It also spins on its axis at a tilted angle. It takes about 24 hours for the Earth to spin around once. As it spins, the side of the Earth that is facing the sun has daylight. The side that is facing away from the sun has nighttime. And for the half of the year that the Northern Hemisphere tilts toward the sun, daylight there is longer than darkness.

Skill Look for a generalization in this paragraph. The word *often* is a clue word.

Skill Find two generalizations in this paragraph. Clue words signal them.

Strategy What could you visualize at this point to help you understand what you read?

Your Turn!

 Need a Review? See the *Envision It!* Skills and Strategies for additional help.

▶ **Ready to Try It?** Use what you've learned about generalizing and visualizing as you read other text.

TEKS
RC-4.D.1 Make inferences about text.
RC-4.D.2 Use textual evidence to support understanding.

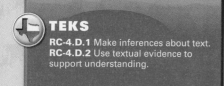

Skill

Strategy

READING STREET ONLINE
ENVISION IT! ANIMATIONS
www.TexasReadingStreet.com

Comprehension Skill

Generalize

- A generalization is a broad statement based on several examples.

- A generalization can be valid (logical) or faulty (wrong) depending on the number of examples on which it is based and on how logical and careful the thinking is.

- When making a generalization, ask yourself if it is supported by facts. A faulty one is not.

- Use the graphic organizer below to help you identify generalizations as you read "Davy Crockett."

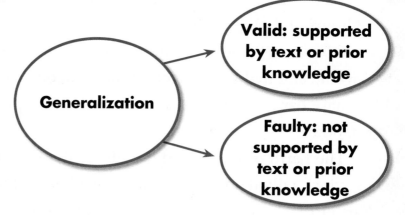

Comprehension Strategy

Inferring

When you infer, you combine your background knowledge with evidence from the text to come up with your own idea about what the author is trying to present. Active readers often infer the ideas, morals, lessons, and themes of a written work.

72

DAVY CROCKETT

David "Davy" Crockett was born on August 17, 1786, in Tennessee. As a young man, Crockett spent a lot of time hunting. Most of the food his family ate came from the animals he hunted. They ate the meat of deer, elk, turkeys, and bears. One year, Crockett said he shot more than fifty bears.

When Crockett was twenty-eight, he fought against the British in the War of 1812. After the war, he explored the forests of Tennessee. In 1821, Davy was elected to the Tennessee congress. He was in office for four years. In 1827, he was elected to the U.S. House of Representatives. After losing in 1831, he ran again in 1833 and won. He stayed in office until 1835.

After leaving office, Davy traveled to Texas. He fought to make Texas independent from Mexico. Crockett was killed during the Battle of the Alamo in March of 1836.

Davy Crockett had the most exciting and interesting life of any frontiersman. He was a skilled rifleman and hunter. He fought in wars and was elected to public office several times.

Skill What clue word signals a generalization? Can it be supported by facts?

Strategy What can you infer about Davy Crockett's personality? Provide evidence to support your answer.

Skill Which statement in this paragraph has a faulty generalization? Explain why.

Your Turn!

 Need a Review? See the *Envision It!* Skills and Strategies for additional help.

Ready to Try It? Use what you've learned about generalizing and inferring as you read other text.

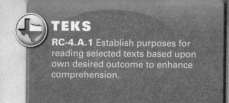

TEKS

RC-4.A.1 Establish purposes for reading selected texts based upon own desired outcome to enhance comprehension.

Envision It! | **Skill Strategy**

Skill

Strategy

READING STREET ONLINE
ENVISION IT! ANIMATIONS
www.TexasReadingStreet.com

Comprehension Skill

Generalize

- A generalization is a broad statement or rule that applies to several examples.

- Authors sometimes use clue words such as *most, all, usually,* and *never* to help readers generalize.

- Some generalizations are valid, or supported by facts and details. Others are faulty, or not supported.

- Use the graphic organizer below to make generalizations as you read "Left in the Dust."

Generalization	Clue Word?

Comprehension Strategy

Predict and Set Purpose

As you read, it is important to make predictions. Your predictions will help you set your purpose for reading. Setting a purpose will guide your reading and help you understand what you read.

Left in the Dust

Sometimes a lot of rain can cause trouble, but not enough rain can cause trouble too. When an area has an extended dry spell, or period of time with an abnormally low amount of rainfall, it is called a drought.

In the 1930s, a severe drought hit Texas and other areas in the American Southwest. Winds that usually brought rain to these areas blew farther south than usual. As a result, not enough rain fell on the farm fields, so no crops could be grown and the dirt in the fields dried up.

The winds blew the dirt up into the air and created blizzardlike dust storms. These storms created dust clouds that blocked out the sun and darkened the skies. One farmer described a storm as being "like a black wall" that went over the area. It was so dry that a news reporter called the area the "Dust Bowl."

America still experiences droughts today, but the long, long dry spell that caused the Dust Bowl is believed to be the worst American drought in more than three hundred years!

Skill There are two generalizations in the first sentence. Identify them and tell whether you agree with them. Explain why or why not.

Skill What can you generalize about the amount of rain that usually falls in the American Southwest?

Strategy Reread the second paragraph. Predict what you will read about next and tell what your purpose for reading will be.

Your Turn!

Need a Review? See the *Envision It!* Skills and Strategies for additional help.

 Ready to Try It? Use what you've learned about generalizing and predicting and setting a purpose as you read other text.

75

Graphic Sources

Graphic sources show information in a way the reader can see.

Table/Chart

Tables and charts are boxes, squares, or rectangles that categorize information in rows and columns.

The Case of the Park Litterbugs

Detective on duty	Day	Garbage found
Jaime	Sunday	9
Jessica	Monday	11
Eric	Tuesday	2
Me	Wednesday	3
Ana Luz	Thursday	5
Milton	Friday	7
Libby	Saturday	15

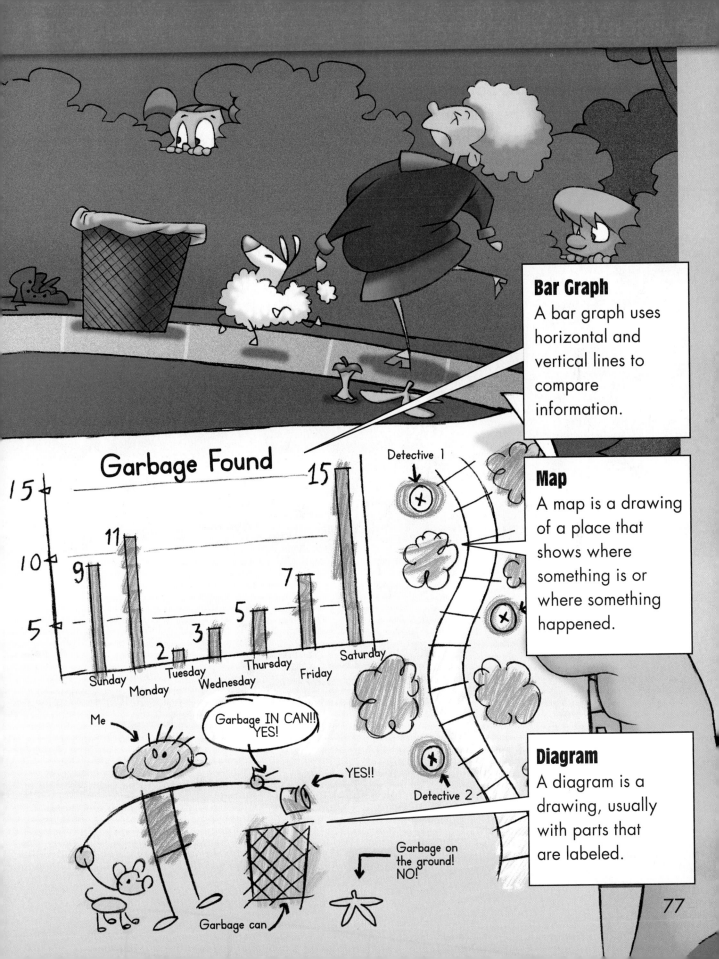

Bar Graph
A bar graph uses horizontal and vertical lines to compare information.

Map
A map is a drawing of a place that shows where something is or where something happened.

Diagram
A diagram is a drawing, usually with parts that are labeled.

77

How to Use Graphic Sources

Charts, diagrams, maps, and graphs are examples of graphic sources, or features. These features can help you understand information or predict what a reading will be about.

See It!

- Look at pages 76–77. What do you notice? What do the images and text tell you about how graphic sources make information easier to understand?

- During reading, scan the text for graphic sources that can help you understand the topic. Look for captions underneath photographs, as well as charts, illustrations, or underlined or boldface words.

- Pick a graphic source to examine in depth. Look at the size, shape, and information given. Is it easy to understand? What does it tell you?

Say It!

- Pause in your reading when you come across graphic sources. Take a few minutes to review the graphic source, and then explain the information aloud with a partner. Does the information make sense? If you or your partner is confused, look back over the graphic source together.

- While reading and examining graphic sources, ask yourself or a partner, "What is the purpose of this graphic? Why would the author choose to include it?"

Do It!

- Make a chart such as the one below to use while reading:

Type of Graphic Source	What It Shows	How It Helps You Understand Information

How do the different graphic sources help you understand information?

- Create your own graphic source to go with something you've written or read. You might choose to create a map, bar graph, text box, or illustration with a caption. Be sure your graphic sources are properly labeled and tell more about your topic.

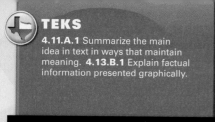

TEKS

4.11.A.1 Summarize the main idea in text in ways that maintain meaning. **4.13.B.1** Explain factual information presented graphically.

Envision It! | Skill Strategy

Skill

Strategy

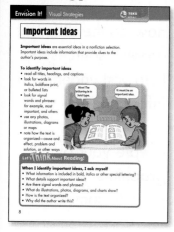

Comprehension Skill

🎯 Graphic Sources

- A graphic source shows or explains information in the text. Illustrations, photographs, maps, diagrams, charts, and time lines are all examples of graphic sources.

- As you read, use graphic sources to help you understand information. Compare information in the text with information in the graphic sources.

- Use the photographs below to help you understand the information in "Measuring the Invisible."

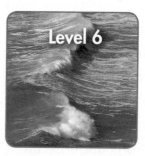

Comprehension Strategy

🎯 Important Ideas

Important ideas are essential ideas and supporting details in a nonfiction selection. Important ideas include information and facts that provide clues to the author's purpose. To identify important ideas, identify all the headings, look for words in special type, and use the graphics in the text.

Measuring the Invisible

How can you measure what you cannot see? For years, people depended on their powers of observation to guess the speed of wind. Today, we have instruments we use to measure wind speed accurately.

One is called an anemometer [an-uh-MOM-i-ter]. As the wind blows past the cups of the anemometer, the cups rotate. The faster the winds blow, the faster the cups rotate. A device then figures out the number of times the cups rotate and turns the information into scientific units of measurement for wind, called knots. One knot is a little more than one mile per hour.

Another instrument is the Beaufort scale. In 1805, a British admiral named Sir Francis Beaufort invented a way to measure wind speed while he was at sea. By watching the effect of wind on the ocean, Beaufort created a scale that classified wind speed from 1 to 12. People changed the scale slightly, but it is still used today to measure wind speed on water, as well as on land.

Skill Look at the photograph of the anemometer at work. Explain how the cups show how fast the wind blows.

Skill Look at the images of Level 2 and Level 6 of the Beaufort scale on the previous page. Which number represents the stronger wind speed?

Strategy Summarize the most important idea of this paragraph.

Your Turn!

Need a Review? See the *Envision It!* Skills and Strategies for additional help.

Ready to Try It? Use what you've learned about graphic sources and important ideas as you read other text.

81

TEKS

RC-4.A.1 Establish purposes for reading selected texts based upon own desired outcome to enhance comprehension. 4.13.B.1 Explain factual information presented graphically.

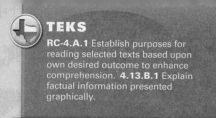

Envision It! | Skill Strategy

Skill

Strategy

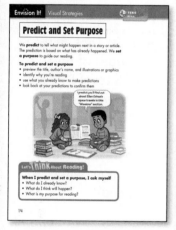

READING STREET ONLINE
ENVISION IT! ANIMATIONS
www.TexasReadingStreet.com

Comprehension Skill

Graphic Sources

- A graphic, such as a chart, diagram, graph, or illustration, can help you organize factual information.

- As you read, use graphic sources to help you understand information. Compare information in the text with information in the graphic.

- Use what you learned about graphic sources as you read "Picture This." Then draw this Egyptian cartouche. Write your first name in the cartouche in hieroglyphics. Place your name and all of your classmates' names in a box. Pick one and use the chart on page 83 to discover whose cartouche you have.

Comprehension Strategy

Predict and Set Purpose

Before they read, good readers look over an article to predict what it is about. Predicting helps good readers set a purpose for reading, such as to be entertained or to be informed. Setting a purpose helps readers determine how they should read the text.

Picture This

In ancient Egypt, people used a form of picture writing known as **hieroglyphics.** This word means "sacred writing." Hieroglyphics were carved on the walls of temples, tombs, and cartouches—oval figures that contained the names of rulers in hieroglyphics.

English writing is made up of letters. The letters represent the sounds of the language. Hieroglyphics were just pictures—no letters at all! Sometimes a picture stood for the thing it showed. For example, sometimes 〰️ meant "water." Other times 〰️ stood for the sound /nnn/ from the Egyptian word for *water*. This chart shows hiero- glyphics that can be used for English letters.

Strategy Look at the chart below. Predict what the passage will be about. Consider the purpose of the chart and how it will help you understand the text.

Skill How does this information relate to the chart below?

Skill Which hieroglyphic can be used for the letter *d*? Which letters have the same hieroglyphic?

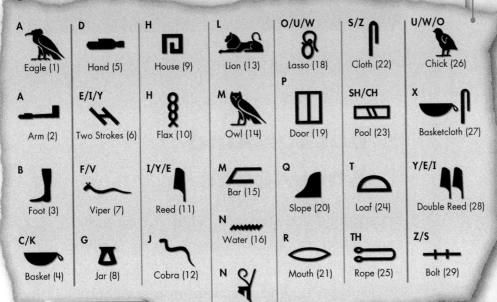

A Eagle (1)	**D** Hand (5)	**H** House (9)	**L** Lion (13)	**O/U/W** Lasso (18)	**S/Z** Cloth (22)	**U/W/O** Chick (26)
A Arm (2)	**E/I/Y** Two Strokes (6)	**H** Flax (10)	**M** Owl (14)	**P** Door (19)	**SH/CH** Pool (23)	**X** Basketcloth (27)
B Foot (3)	**F/V** Viper (7)	**I/Y/E** Reed (11)	**M** Bar (15)	**Q** Slope (20)	**T** Loaf (24)	**Y/E/I** Double Reed (28)
C/K Basket (4)	**G** Jar (8)	**J** Cobra (12)	**N** Water (16)	**R** Mouth (21)	**TH** Rope (25)	**Z/S** Bolt (29)
			N Crown (17)			

Your Turn!

⏸ **Need a Review?** See the *Envision It!* Skills and Strategies for additional help.

▶ **Ready to Try It?** Use what you've learned about graphic sources and predicting and setting a purpose as you read other text.

Envision It! | Skill Strategy

Skill

Strategy

Comprehension Skill

Graphic Sources

- A graphic source, such as a chart, diagram, graph, or illustration, helps you organize information so it is easier to understand.

- Use graphic sources and text features as you read to help you understand and locate information. Compare information in the text with information in the graphic.

- Use the diagram on the next page and the photograph below to organize the information presented in "The Other Side of the Moon."

Phases of the Moon

Comprehension Strategy

Background Knowledge

Background knowledge is what you already know about a topic or subject. Good readers use their background knowledge to monitor and adjust their reading. Previewing a selection will help you determine what knowledge you will bring to a selection. You can use background knowledge while you read, especially if you come across information you don't understand.

The Other Side of the Moon

There is one side of the moon—called the far side—that no one standing on the Earth has ever seen. Astronauts have gone behind the moon to see the other side. However, no one simply looking up at the sky has ever seen the back of the moon.

Why?

The answer lies in the way the moon moves. The moon orbits Earth, but it also turns once on its axis in the same amount of time. This is called synchronous rotation.

Study the diagram below.

Imagine you went to the moon and painted a crater red to serve as a marker. Then you came back to Earth and looked up at the moon night after night. If the moon did not rotate, your marker would seem to move across the moon and even disappear for a while as the moon orbited Earth. But your red crater stays in sight, which means that the moon rotates and shows us only one side.

Moon's rotation on its axis

Moon's orbit of Earth

Skill Preview the title and the diagram on this page. Explain how you think this diagram can help you to understand the passage.

Strategy What do you already know about this topic? How does this knowledge help you to understand the information in the passage?

Skill Do you think this sentence is important for the author to include in the passage? Explain why or why not.

Your Turn!

Need a Review? See the *Envision It!* Skills and Strategies for additional help.

 Ready to Try It? Use what you've learned about graphic sources and background knowledge as you read other text.

Room To Grow

Literary Elements

Stories are made up of four main elements: character, setting, plot, and theme. Each of these parts gives you an overall understanding of the story.

Characters

A character is a person or an animal in a story.

Setting

The setting is the time and place in which a story happens.

Plot

The plot is the pattern of events in a story.

The plot starts with a problem or goal and builds toward a climax. The plot ends with a resolution or outcome.

Theme

The theme is the big idea of a story. We look at the plot, setting, or characters to determine the theme of a story.

How to Identify Literary Elements

Stories are made up of the following parts: characters, setting, plot, and theme.

See It!

- Look at pages 86–87. What information do the pictures give you? Explain.

- Look for hints about a story's characters, setting, theme, or plot in the illustrations or other graphic elements of a text. How are the characters shown in the illustrations? What do the illustrations tell you about the time and place?

- Visualize as you read an author's descriptions of characters and setting. Try to picture in your mind what the author is describing.

Say It!

- With a partner, read aloud pages 86–87. What do you learn about characters, setting, theme, and plot? Look at the images before and after you read each description.

- Think about a story or movie you have seen recently. Tell a partner what the characters, setting, theme, and plot of the story are. If you have difficulty with the theme, think about what the most important idea of the story is in your own words. Remember, there can be more than one theme to a story.

Do It!

- Make a list of important events. What problems do the characters encounter? How are those problems solved?

- Draw a story's characters or setting and include a caption underneath that gives a brief description.

- Make a graphic organizer like the one below to help you identify story events and plot:

TEKS

4.6.B.1 Describe the interaction of characters including their relationships. 4.6.B.2 Describe the interaction of characters including the changes they undergo. RC-4.C.1 Monitor comprehension. RC-4.C.2 Adjust comprehension.

Envision It! | Skill Strategy

Skill

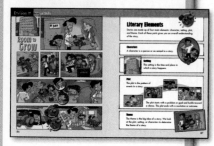

Strategy

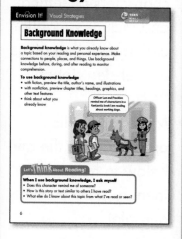

**READING STREET ONLINE
ENVISION IT! ANIMATIONS**
www.TexasReadingStreet.com

Comprehension Skill

Literary Elements: Character, Setting, and Plot

- Characters are the people in a story. We learn what characters are like by noticing how they act and what they say in the story.

- When a character tells the story using *I, me,* and *my,* the author is writing in the first person. If events are told by a narrator who is not in the story, using *he, him, his, she,* and *her,* the author is writing in the third person.

- The setting of a story is where it takes place and when it happens.

- The plot is the sequence of events in a story.

- Use the chart to identify characters, setting, and plot as you read "The 'Broken' Arm."

Characters	Setting	Plot

Comprehension Strategy

Background Knowledge

Good readers use what they know to help them understand a story. Before reading, look at the title and pictures. If you know something about the subject matter of the story, it will help you understand what you are reading.

90

The "Broken" Arm

Eliza and her sister Harriet took turns washing the dishes. When Harriet did the dishes, Eliza played the fiddle or did her homework. When Eliza did the dishes, Harriet would sit with her father and watch the stars.

One night Eliza was limping when she came in from doing her chores. It was her night to do the dishes.

"My ankle! It hurts!" she cried. Pa looked at it.

"Don't worry," Pa said. "It's not broken. But you need to stay off it. Harriet can do the dishes tonight."

Pa sat with Eliza for the rest of the night, soothing her and bandaging her ankle.

Harriet scowled every time she placed a dish in the rack—she just boiled up inside. Then she got an idea.

The next night, Harriet came into the house crying.

"Ow, Pa. My arm hurts!"

"What's wrong?" Pa asked.

"My arm! I think it's broken!"

Pa looked at the arm. He knew he wouldn't find any broken bones because Harriet had just spent the last hour lying in the grass looking at the clouds.

"Does it really hurt, Harriet?" Pa said, with a doubtful smile on his face. Harriet knew her father well. She knew she couldn't fool him. "Well," she said as her arm dropped to her side. "I guess I'd rather do the dishes than really have a broken arm!"

Skill Describe the interactions of Eliza and Harriet. Describe their relationship. Is this story told in the first or third person?

Strategy Does knowing that Harriet and Eliza switched off every night to do the dishes help you understand how Harriet felt?

Skill Describe how Harriet feels at the end of this story. Explain how she has changed.

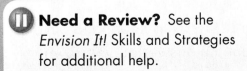

Your Turn!

 Need a Review? See the *Envision It!* Skills and Strategies for additional help.

▶ **Ready to Try It?** Use what you've learned about literary elements and background knowledge as you read other text.

91

TEKS
4.6.A.1 Sequence the plot's main events. **4.6.B.2** Describe the interaction of characters including the changes they undergo. **RC-4.C.1** Monitor comprehension. **RC-4.C.2** Adjust comprehension.

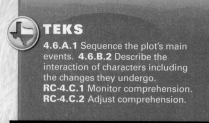

Envision It! | Skill Strategy

Skill

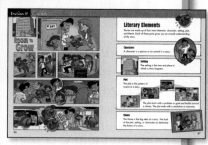

Strategy

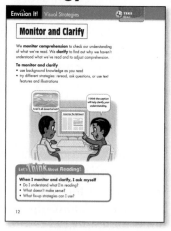

READING STREET ONLINE
ENVISION IT! ANIMATIONS
www.TexasReadingStreet.com

Comprehension Skill

Literary Elements: Character and Plot

- A character is a person or animal who takes part in a story. You can learn about a character through the character's words and thoughts. You can also learn about a character through the author's description of the character's relationships.

- A plot is the series of sequenced, related events in a story. The plot includes the conflict, or problem; the rising action; the climax; and the resolution, or outcome.

- Use a graphic organizer like this one to identify the events of the plot in "Oh, No!"

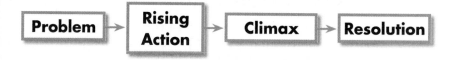

| Problem | → | Rising Action | → | Climax | → | Resolution |

Comprehension Strategy

Monitor and Clarify

When you are reading, it's important for you to monitor when you understand something and when you don't. If you are confused, stop and reread the section aloud. Looking back and rereading is one way to clarify, or "adjust," your understanding. Asking an interpretive question of text is another way. An interpretive question is answered by using information in the text to figure out the answer on your own.

Catherine was very excited when she learned that both she and her friend Shelly had gotten parts in the play. She had always wanted to act. Mr. Kiley, the director, explained that it was important for everyone to attend each rehearsal.

On Day 4 of rehearsals, Catherine felt feverish. That night her fever was high, and the next day she stayed in bed.

The doctor told Catherine that she would probably miss a week of school. "Oh, *no!* I can't miss that much!" she cried. "I'll be replaced in the class play."

That evening Catherine heard the telephone ring. Several minutes later her mother came into her bedroom.

"That was Mr. Kiley on the telephone," she said.

"He called to tell me I've been replaced, no doubt," Catherine moaned, suddenly feeling worse.

"No," said her mother. "He asked if Shelly could visit you after each rehearsal to keep you informed. Then you'll be able to catch up when you get back next week."

"Oh, *yes!*" Catherine screamed excitedly and jumped up.

"Hey!" laughed her mother. "Do you want your fever to *ever* go down?"

Skill What do you think Catherine's problem is going to be?

Strategy Why does Catherine think Mr. Kiley will replace her in the play? Stop and reread aloud the beginning of the selection to clarify why Catherine thinks this.

Skill The problem is resolved here. How has Catherine changed from the beginning of the story?

Your Turn!

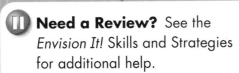

Need a Review? See the *Envision It!* Skills and Strategies for additional help.

Ready to Try It? Use what you've learned about character and plot and monitoring and clarifying as you read other text.

TEKS

4.3.A.1 Summarize the lesson or message of a work of fiction as its theme. **4.6.A.1** Sequence the plot's main events. **4.6.A.3** Explain the plot's main events' influence on future events. **Also 4.6.B.1.**

Envision It! | Skill Strategy

Skill

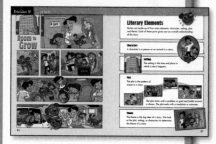

Strategy

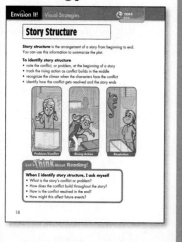

**READING STREET ONLINE
ENVISION IT! ANIMATIONS**
www.TexasReadingStreet.com

Comprehension Skill

Literary Elements: Character, Plot, and Theme

- **Characters** are the people in a story. Readers learn about characters by what they say and how they act.

- A **plot** is the sequence of events in a story. Events that happen in the story move the plot forward.

- A story's **theme** is the most important idea. When you finish reading, ask yourself *What does this story mean? What is it all about?*

- Use the graphic to identify the characters, plot, and theme of "A Family Just Like Ours."

Character	Plot	Theme

Comprehension Strategy

Story Structure

Readers pay attention to story structure, or how a fictional story is put together. As you read, notice how the story begins, how it builds through the middle, and how it ends. Events that take place throughout the story move the plot to its logical conclusion.

A Family
Just Like Ours

Madeline rolled over in her sleeping bag. Blinking, she looked at her mom, wide awake and curled up in a sleeping bag in their tent. "Good morning, Maddy."

"Morning, Mom."

Maddy and her mother left their tent in Grand Teton National Park, Wyoming. Maddy peeked into her dad and brother's tent. She could hear snoring.

"Let's let them sleep. How about a walk?" Mom whispered, handing Maddy a water bottle.

They trekked past the edge of the campsite. Suddenly, Mom stopped. She touched Maddy lightly on the shoulder, put her finger against her lips as a sign for quiet, and pointed toward the stream.

There stood a huge bull moose with a giant rack of antlers, a smaller female moose, and a baby moose. The mother moose walked into the stream, nudging the baby moose along with her. The baby moose splashed in the water, just like Maddy's little brother might have done. Maddy laughed.

The mother moose must have heard her. Turning her head, the moose looked in their direction. The father moose began herding his family away.

Skill Describe the interactions of the characters and their relationships.

Strategy What events have happened so far? Explain how the mother's sign for quiet results in the next event in the plot.

Skill What is this story about? Summarize the story's theme. Have the characters changed? Explain.

Your Turn!

⏸ Need a Review? See the *Envision It!* Skills and Strategies for additional help.

 Ready to Try It? As you read other text, use what you've learned about literary elements and story structure to help you understand it.

Main Idea and Details

Main idea is the most important idea about a topic. Details support the main idea.

How to Identify Main Idea and Details

The main idea is what a story is mostly about. Details are the pieces of information that tell more about the main idea or help explain it.

See It!

- Look at page 96. What details are pictured? What do you think is the main idea? Why? How do the details of the picture help you understand this main idea? Explain.

- Use illustrations, graphs, and other images from your reading to help you figure out the main idea of the story. What kind of information do you get from the images? How does this help you tell the main idea?

Say It!

- With a partner, state the main idea of your reading. Each of you should come up with at least one example from the reading that supports, or proves, this statement. If you cannot do this, you may have not correctly identified the main idea.

- To check if you have correctly identified the main idea, tell it to a partner after reading. Ask him or her: "Does my main idea make sense? Does it cover all the important details?"

Do It!

- Use a web like the one below to identify main idea and details.

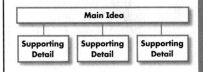

- Think about your favorite movie or book, and why you like it. Write a paragraph where you give at least three examples of why this movie or book is one of your favorites. When you're done writing, circle the main idea and underline the details that tell more about it. Do all details support the main idea?

TEKS

4.11.A.1 Summarize the main idea in text in ways that maintain meaning. **4.11.A.2** Summarize the supporting details in text in ways that maintain meaning. **Also 4.11.C.1, 4.11.C.2, 4.11.C.3.**

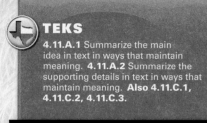

Envision It! | Skill Strategy

Skill

Strategy

READING STREET ONLINE
ENVISION IT! ANIMATIONS
www.TexasReadingStreet.com

Comprehension Skill

🎯 Main Idea and Details

- The topic is what a paragraph, part of an article, or a whole article is about.

- The most important thing an author has to say about the topic is the main idea.

- The pieces of information that tell more about the main idea are the supporting details.

- Use the graphic organizer to summarize main idea and supporting details as you read "Send a Ranger."

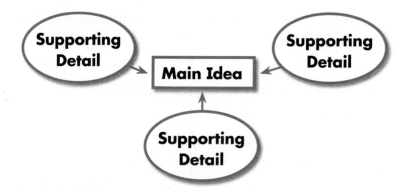

Comprehension Strategy

🎯 Text Structure

Understanding the way a text is organized can help you understand what you are reading. Before you read, preview the text and look for text features such as titles, headings, underlined words, and clue words (words that show cause and effect, sequence, or compare and contrast), to help you know what to expect.

SEND A RANGER!

The job of a ranger is made up of different jobs. Park rangers are like police officers—they make sure people obey the rules of the park. Park rangers are like teachers—they take people on nature walks and tell them about important places in our history. Park rangers are like scientists—they keep track of information about plants and animals. Park rangers are like firefighters—they keep close watch to help put a stop to forest fires. Park rangers are like rescue workers—they hunt for people who are lost or hurt.

Skill Summarize the details you learned about a ranger's job. Summarize the main idea of this paragraph.

Yes, the job of a park ranger is made up of many different jobs. In fact, Stephen Mather, the first director of the National Parks Service, has said: "If a trail is to be blazed, send a ranger; if an animal is floundering in the snow, send a ranger; if a bear is in a hotel, send a ranger; if a fire threatens a forest, send a ranger; and if someone is to be saved, send a ranger."

Skill Why do you think the author restated a sentence used earlier? Is this a clue about what the main idea is?

Strategy Can you find a comparison the author used to describe the job of a ranger?

Does this sound like fun to you? Maybe you would like to be a park ranger.

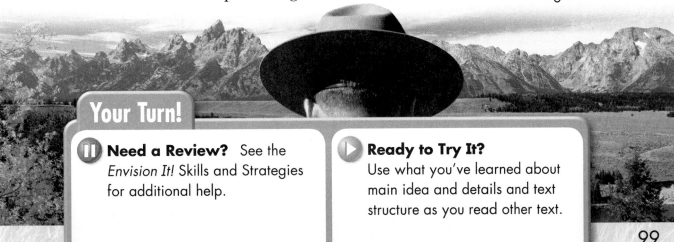

Your Turn!

Need a Review? See the *Envision It!* Skills and Strategies for additional help.

Ready to Try It? Use what you've learned about main idea and details and text structure as you read other text.

TEKS

4.11.A.1 Summarize the main idea in text in ways that maintain meaning. **4.11.A.2** Summarize the supporting details in text in ways that maintain meaning. **RC-4.D.1** Make inferences about text. **Also RC-4.D.2.**

Envision It! Skill Strategy

Skill

Strategy

Comprehension Skill

🎯 Main Idea and Details

- The focus of a paragraph or an article is the topic, or what the paragraph or article is about.

- The most important thing an author has to say about the topic is the main idea.

- Small pieces of information that tell more about the main idea are supporting details.

- Use the graphic organizer to summarize the main idea and details in "A White House History."

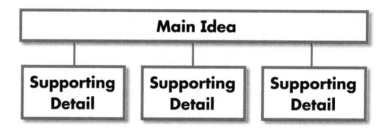

Comprehension Strategy

🎯 Inferring

When you infer, you combine your background knowledge with clues in the text to come up with your own idea about what the author is writing about. Good readers often infer the ideas, morals, lessons, and themes of a story or an article.

A WHITE HOUSE HISTORY

The White House, in Washington, D.C., is where the President of the United States lives and works. Although our first President, George Washington, chose the spot where the White House would be built, he never even lived there! The building began in 1792, but it wasn't finished until Washington was out of office. •

Skill Summarize the main idea of the first paragraph. Find a detail that supports it.

Our second President, John Adams, moved into the White House in 1800. The building still wasn't finished. As a result, it was somewhat uncomfortable for daily life. The President's wife, Abigail, had nowhere to hang the family's laundry, so she used the East Room. Today that room is the biggest, grandest room in the White House. •

Strategy What clues in the text can you use to help you infer what the East Room might be used for today?

In 1814, while our fourth President, James Madison, was in office, the United States was again at war with England. The British burned the White House, and it had to be rebuilt. •

Skill Summarize the main idea of the third paragraph. Find a detail that supports it.

By 1902, so many people worked in the White House that Theodore Roosevelt built the West Wing. The new wing freed up space for his six lively children and their pets.

Even though Presidents live in the White House, it really belongs to the American people.

Your Turn!

 Need a Review? See the *Envision It!* Skills and Strategies for additional help.

▶ **Ready to Try It?** Use what you've learned about main idea and details and inferring as you read other text.

TEKS

4.11.A.1 Summarize the main idea in text in ways that maintain meaning. **4.11.A.2** Summarize the supporting details in text in ways that maintain meaning. **4.11.D.1** Use multiple text features to gain an overview of the contents of text.

Envision It! | Skill Strategy

Skill

Strategy

READING STREET ONLINE
ENVISION IT! ANIMATIONS
www.TexasReadingStreet.com

Comprehension Skill

Main Idea and Details

- A topic is what a piece of writing is about.

- The main idea is the most important idea about the topic.

- Supporting details give information about the main idea.

- Use the graphic organizer to summarize both main idea and details as you read "Glaciers and Icebergs."

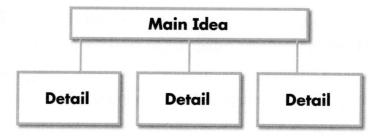

Comprehension Strategy

Text Structure

Text structure helps readers understand what they read. For example, a nonfiction article may compare and contrast two things, put events in sequence, or be a series of main ideas. When you preview, look for text features such as headings, guide words in bold print, and underlined words to help you know what to expect.

Glaciers and Icebergs

Glaciers and icebergs are both made of ice and are both very large.

Glaciers Glaciers are huge pieces of ice that are on land. They are found in areas where there is steady snowfall. Glaciers form when more snow falls than melts away over the years. The leftover snow slowly recrystallizes to form ice.

Types of Glaciers There are two types of glaciers. Mountain glaciers move down the sides of mountains. Ice sheets, on the other hand, form on level ground and spread out in all directions. The continent of Antarctica is covered by a huge ice sheet.

Icebergs Some glaciers or ice sheets go all the way to the seashore. As the ice reaches the shore, a part of it may break off and fall into the sea. This huge piece of ice, now floating in the ocean, is called an iceberg. About 10,000 icebergs each year come from the glaciers that cover Greenland.

Skill Summarize the main idea of this paragraph. Summarize the details that support that idea.

Strategy Which text structure is used in this paragraph? How can you tell?
A. sequence
B. compare and contrast
C. main idea

Skill Explain where you would find information about ice sheets. What text feature tells you?

Your Turn!

 Need a Review? See the *Envision It!* Skills and Strategies for additional help.

Ready to Try It? Use what you've learned about main idea and details and text structure as you read other text.

Sequence

Sequence refers to the order of events in text. We also use sequence when we list the steps in a process.

104

How to Identify Sequence

The sequence is the order in which things happen in a story—what happens first, next, and last.

See It!

- Look for clue words, such as *first, next, then,* or *after.* They will help tell you the order of a story.

- Look at the image on page 104. What do you see happening first, next, and last? Tell the sequence to a partner.

- Does the story have illustrations or other images? If so, do they give you any clues about what happens first, next, and last? Use the pictures to help you understand sequence as you read.

Say It!

- Take turns telling a partner what happens first, next, and last in the story.

- Retell what has been read by asking, "What have I just read?" Summarize the events. Do this when you feel confused or haven't read the story for a few days—it will help you remember and identify what happened first, next, and last.

- Some authors tell a story out of sequence. Ask a classmate to paraphrase, or tell in his or her own words, what happened in the story from beginning to end.

Do It!

- On a sheet of paper or a computer program, draw images that match the story's events. Be sure to put your illustrations in order of first, next, and last to identify sequence.

- Make a sequence diagram or a time line to help you keep track of the story's most important events:

- In groups, perform skits. Each group should take a different part of the story to act out. Groups then should perform the skits in the order of events.

TEKS

4.6.A.1 Sequence the plot's main events. **4.6.A.2** Summarize the plot's main events.

Envision It! | Skill Strategy

Skill

Strategy

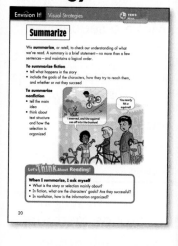

Comprehension Skill

Sequence

- Events in a story occur in a certain order, or sequence. The sequence of events can be important to understanding the story.

- Sometimes an author tells the events in a story out of sequence. When an author does this, an event that happened earlier in a story might be told *after* an event that happened later.

- It will help you figure out what is happening in a story if you stop and summarize the events that have taken place so far.

- Use the graphic organizer to sequence and summarize the plot of "Going Batty."

Main Event   **Main Event**

Main Event   **Main Event**

Comprehension Strategy

Summarize

Good readers summarize information as they read. When you read, identify the important ideas and briefly retell them in your own words. As you summarize, notice whether your thoughts about what you are reading change.

Going Batty

Mrs. Koch's fourth-grade class walked to the library, just as they did every afternoon. At the door, their mouths dropped open. Hanging everywhere were bats—upside-down, black bats. It took a few seconds before they realized the bats were paper. "Why all the bats?" they asked Mr. Egan, the librarian.

Mr. Egan laughed. "We had some excitement this morning." He went on to explain.

"The day started quietly. I checked in some books. Then a kindergarten class arrived for Story Hour. They sat in a circle while I began reading *Stellaluna*. It's about a little fruit bat. Well, suddenly the children yelled, 'Stellaluna! Stellaluna!' I love it when children get excited about a story, but this was ridiculous! Then I saw they were pointing up. A bat was in the library! I was able to trap it in a box and take it outside. The children made paper bats to take its place."

The fourth graders looked around hopefully. But there were no real bats. Sometimes kindergarten children have all the luck.

Skill Which grade is mentioned first in the story? Why do you suppose this should not be the first event on your graphic organizer?

Skill What time-word clues tell you that Mr. Egan is going to tell about events that happened earlier in the day?

Strategy Give a brief summary about the important events in paragraph three.

Your Turn!

 Need a Review? See the *Envision It!* Skills and Strategies for additional help.

▶ **Ready to Try It?** Use what you've learned about sequencing and summarizing as you read other text.

TEKS

4.11.A.1 Summarize the main idea in text in ways that maintain meaning. **4.11.C.2** Describe explicit relationships among ideas in texts organized by sequence. **4.11.C.5** Describe implicit relationships among ideas in texts organized by sequence.

Envision It! | Skill Strategy

Skill

Strategy

READING STREET ONLINE
ENVISION IT! ANIMATIONS
www.TexasReadingStreet.com

Comprehension Skill

Sequence

- Sequence is the order in which relationships among ideas happen in a text. Sequence can also mean the steps people follow to do something.

- You can identify explicit sequence relationships because clue words such as *first, then, next, after,* and *last* tell you the order of the events.

- If the sequence is implicit, there may not be any clue words. You will have to figure out the order of the events on your own.

- Words such as *while, meanwhile,* and *during* can show when events happen at the same time.

- Use this graphic organizer to figure out the explicit and implicit sequence of events in "Merril Sandoval: The Life of a Code Talker."

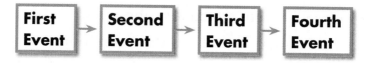

| First Event | → | Second Event | → | Third Event | → | Fourth Event |

Comprehension Strategy

Important Ideas

Important ideas are the essential ideas in a text. While reading a nonfiction text, try to identify the most important ideas an author has to say about the topic. You can use the subheads, photographs, and illustrations to help you identify the important ideas. Then try to notice the difference between important ideas and interesting details.

Merril Sandoval:
THE LIFE OF A CODE TALKER

Merril Sandoval was a freshman at Farmington Mission School in New Mexico when Marines visited his school. They were looking for young Navajo men to train as code talkers—Navajos who sent and received secret coded messages during World War II. Merril wanted to join, but he was only sixteen years old. Samuel, Merril's older brother, was able to join. So Merril stayed in school, and Samuel left with the Marines.

In March 1943, during Merril's second year in high school, he was old enough to become a Marine. He was excited to be part of the Navajo code-talking program.

From March through June, Merril attended boot camp in California for basic training. After boot camp, he went to communications school to learn how to use and fix radios.

On February 19, 1945, Merril was sent to Iwo Jima, Japan. While there, he translated reports from code talkers on the island. Then he sent back the important messages to the military in Hawaii.

After his discharge from the Marine Corps in March 1946, Merril finished high school.

Skill Sometimes two events happen at the same time. What event took place while Merril was still in school?

Strategy What important idea about the topic is in this paragraph?

Skill Which of the following events took place first? How do you know?
(a) Merril learned how to use a radio.
(b) Merril went to boot camp.
(c) Merril finished high school.

Your Turn!

Need a Review? See the *Envision It!* Skills and Strategies for additional help.

Ready to Try It? Use what you've learned about sequencing and important ideas as you read other text.

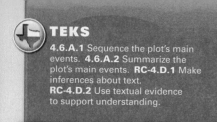

TEKS

4.6.A.1 Sequence the plot's main events. **4.6.A.2** Summarize the plot's main events. **RC-4.D.1** Make inferences about text. **RC-4.D.2** Use textual evidence to support understanding.

Envision It! Skill Strategy

Skill

Strategy

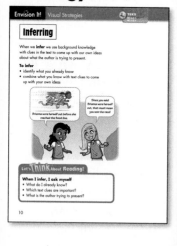

READING STREET ONLINE
ENVISION IT! ANIMATIONS
www.TexasReadingStreet.com

Comprehension Skill

Sequence

- Sequence is the order in which events happen in a story. The order of events may be explicit, and clue words such as *first*, *before*, and *after* signal the sequence. Or the sequence may be implicit, and there are no clue words. The reader has to figure out which events came first, next, and last.

- A story's plot has a sequence of main events. Sometimes main events are told out of sequence. Something that happened earlier might be told after something that happened later.

- Use the graphic organizer to sequence the main events of the plot and to describe explicit and implicit relationships among the ideas in "Dare to Dream," a text organized by sequence. Then summarize the story.

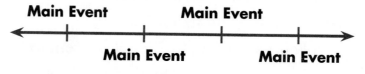

Comprehension Strategy

Inferring

When you infer, you combine your background knowledge with evidence in the text to come up with your own idea about what the author is trying to present. Active readers infer the ideas, morals, lessons, and themes of a written work.

Dare to Dream

Ever since he was a little boy, Rico was one of the best young baseball players in the Dominican Republic. Carlos was sure that one day his big brother would play for a major league team.

Though Rico was eighteen and Carlos was ten, they were best buddies. For the past four years, Carlos has gone to every one of Rico's games. But today there was no game—there was something much more important. Rico was trying out for one of the baseball training camps that are run by major league teams from the United States.

Skill What is the story's first main event?

The weeks before the tryouts, Rico worked harder than usual. "If you want to make it," Rico told Carlos, "don't give up. Always dare to dream."

Finally, the big day arrived. Rico was nervous, and so was Carlos. But Carlos knew that his brother was ready. He had worked too hard. This was going to be his brother's next big step.

Strategy What can you infer about Carlos and his relationship with his brother? How does Carlos feel about his big brother?

The very next day, Carlos was the first to hear the happy news from Rico. He was going to training camp! Dreams *can* come true, thought Carlos—especially if you help them along with hard work.

Skill What is the story's last main event? Explain whether the sequence was explicit or implicit.

Your Turn!

 Need a Review? See the *Envision It!* Skills and Strategies for additional help.

▶ **Ready to Try It?** As you read other text, use what you've learned about sequencing and inferring to help you understand it.

Categorize and Classify

When we categorize and classify, we look at how people or things are related based on their characteristics.

How to Categorize and Classify

When we categorize and classify, we look at how people or things are related based on their characteristics.

See It!

- Look at page 112. What do you see? How does the picture help you understand how to categorize and classify?

- Put the items below into related groups:

- Look at items around the classroom. What things are related to each other? With a partner, make a list of the things you see that you can put into groups.

Say It!

- Picture a place you have been before, such as a park, grocery store, or school. With a partner, name aloud things that you see there. For example, you might see apples, bananas, milk, and juice at a grocery store. Take turns naming items aloud and placing them into groups.

- Look around the classroom. What things do you see that you can put into a group? Why? With a partner, name and describe aloud related items. Be sure to explain why these items belong in a group together.

Do It!

- Make a graphic organizer like the one below:

Common Characteristic		
Thing 1	Thing 2	Thing 3

- With your teacher, gather small items around the classroom that you can easily classify and categorize. These can include things you write with or write on, shapes, things you read, and so on. Sort the objects in any of the following ways: by shape, by color, by how you use them, and so on.

- Test yourself by looking for things at home that you can classify and categorize.

Vocabulary Skills and Strategies

Vocabulary skills and strategies are tools you use to help you figure out the meanings of words. Knowing the meanings of vocabulary will help you better understand what you read.

As you read, if you come to a word that you do not know,

- know when to use word parts to figure out its meaning.
- know when to use words in the surrounding text to figure out its meaning.
- know when to use a dictionary or glossary to figure out its meaning.

Ready to Try It?

WORDS! | Vocabulary

Related Words

Context Clues

Antonyms

Synonyms

Prefixes

Suffixes

Dictionary

Thesaurus

Multiple-Meaning Words

Homographs

Homonyms

Homophones

Base Words/Root Words

Word Origins: Roots

Related Words

Related words all have the same base word.

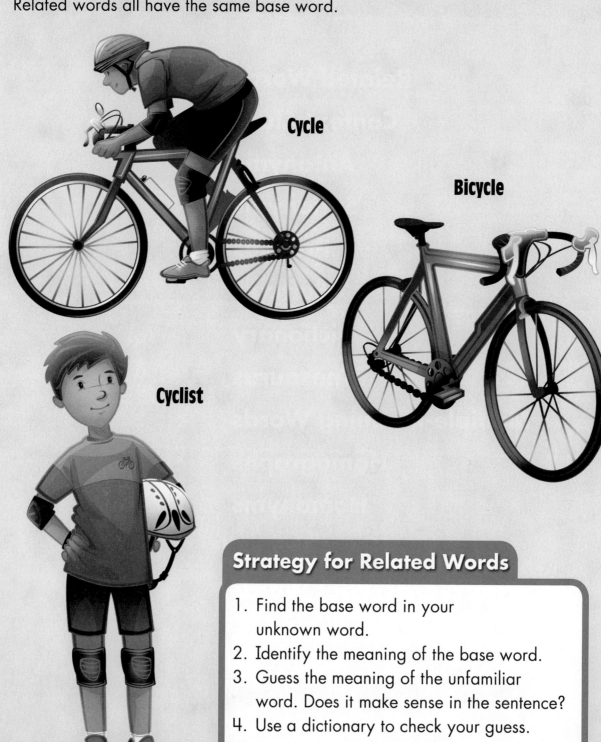

Cycle

Bicycle

Cyclist

Strategy for Related Words

1. Find the base word in your unknown word.
2. Identify the meaning of the base word.
3. Guess the meaning of the unfamiliar word. Does it make sense in the sentence?
4. Use a dictionary to check your guess.

Context Clues

Context clues are the words and sentences found around an unknown word that can help you understand the word's meaning. Use context clues to figure out what a fireworm is.

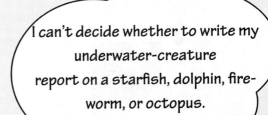

I can't decide whether to write my underwater-creature report on a starfish, dolphin, fire-worm, or octopus.

Strategy for Context Clues

1. Look for clues in the words and phrases around the unknown word.
2. Take a guess at the word's meaning. Does it make sense in the sentence?
3. Use a dictionary to check your guess.

TEKS

4.2.B.1 Use the context of the sentence to determine meaning of an unfamiliar word.

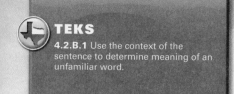

Envision It! Words to Know

brilliant

chorus

shimmering

coward

gleamed

READING STREET ONLINE
VOCABULARY ACTIVITIES
www.TexasReadingStreet.com

Vocabulary Strategy for

🎯 Unfamiliar Words

Context Clues Sometimes when you read, you come to a word you do not know. The context, or the words and sentences around the unfamiliar word, may give you clues to the word's meaning.

1. Read the words and sentences around the unfamiliar word. The author may have included a definition, a synonym, or another clue to the word's meaning.

2. If not, say what the sentence means in your own words.

3. Predict a meaning for the unfamiliar word.

4. Try that meaning in the sentence to see if it makes sense.

Read "At the Edge of the Sea." Use context clues to help you determine the meanings of unfamiliar words.

Words to Write Reread "At the Edge of the Sea." Imagine you are on the coast of a tropical sea. Write a letter home describing what you see and how you feel. Use words from the *Words to Know* list in your writing.

At the Edge of the Sea

The two boys hesitated at the edge of the forest. They looked out at the sea. Waves caught the morning sun and sparkled in a thousand points like brilliant jewels. The white sand gleamed as though some servant of the wind had been polishing it all night. The boys knew it would soon be too hot to tread.

Still, they stood gazing out. The scene was like a painting. Its colors were bright and already shimmering with heat. Other than the waves and a few seabirds, nothing moved. It was all too radiant. Perhaps it also did not seem real because a great journey lay ahead of them. They hoped for some omen of good luck.

At their backs, a chorus of birds began their songs. "May your travels be safe," they seemed to chant. "May your hearts be true and brave. May you never know the shame of a coward. Firm in purpose, may you find what you seek."

The boys smiled then. They shifted the canoe on their shoulders and stepped forward onto the white sand.

Your Turn!

⏸ **Need a Review?** For help with using context clues to determine the meanings of unfamiliar words, see page 117.

▶ **Ready to Try It?** As you read other text, use context clues to help you determine the meanings of unfamiliar words.

TEKS

4.2.B.1 Use the context of the sentence to determine meaning of an unfamiliar word.

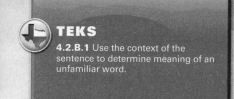

Envision It! | Words to Know

coil

rappel

ridge

descent

foresaw

shaft

trekked

void

Vocabulary Strategy for

🎯 Unfamiliar Words

Context Clues Sometimes you can use context clues, or the words in sentences around an unfamiliar word, to help you figure out its meaning.

1. Read the words and sentences around the unfamiliar word to see if the author has given you a definition of the word.

2. If not, say what the sentence means in your own words.

3. Predict a meaning for the unfamiliar word.

4. Try that meaning in the sentence to see if it makes sense.

5. If the context clues don't help, you can look up the word in a glossary or dictionary.

As you read "Climbing New Heights," use context clues to help you figure out the meanings of this week's *Words to Know.*

Words to Write Reread "Climbing New Heights." Imagine that Mr. Dunn is coming to speak to your class. Make a list of questions that you would like to ask him about his experiences mountain climbing. Use words from the *Words to Know* list in your questions.

CLIMBING NEW HEIGHTS

George Dunn has trekked across flat glaciers and climbed steep mountains for more than thirty years. He grew up in an area around Seattle, Washington. George's parents foresaw their son's lifelong passion to climb up and rappel down mountains.

Dunn is never happier than when facing a ridge of mountains in the distance with a coil of rope over his shoulder. George has climbed to the top of Mount Rainier more times than any other human (480 summits and counting), and he has made a descent from some of the highest peaks in the world. Some of his favorite places to climb are the Swiss Alps and the peaks of Peru.

Dunn likes to share his knowledge and enjoyment of mountain climbing, rock climbing, rappelling, and ice climbing with others. He is an expert guide, and he helps train amateur climbers so that they can experience the feeling of sitting on top of the world. But climbing can be dangerous. Dunn teaches safety and responsibility too. He does not want his students falling into a void between two rocks or down a shaft of a glacier.

Your Turn!

 Need a Review?
For help with using context clues to determine the meanings of unfamiliar words, see page 117.

 Ready to Try It?
As you read other text, use context clues to help you determine the meanings of unfamiliar words.

TEKS

4.2.B.1 Use the context of the
sentence to determine meaning of an
unfamiliar word.

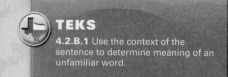

Envision It! Words to Know

colonel

lurking

palettes

affords

glint

quaint

resemblance

Vocabulary Strategy for

🔊 Unfamiliar Words

Context Clues When you read, you may come across a word you are not familiar with. The context of the sentence—the words and sentences around the unfamiliar word—may give you clues to the word's meaning.

1. Read the words and sentences around the unfamiliar word. See if the author has put an example or a definition of the word in parentheses or between commas or dashes in the sentence.

2. If not, say what the sentence means in your own words.

3. Think of a meaning for the unfamiliar word.

4. Try that meaning in the sentence. Determine whether or not it makes sense.

As you read "An Officer and an Artist," use context clues to help you figure out the meanings of *affords* and *glint* and other unfamiliar words.

Words to Write Reread "An Officer and an Artist." Write a description of an interesting person you know. Describe what the person does and why the person is interesting to you. Use words from the *Words to Know* list in your writing.

An Officer and an Artist

My great-uncle Bob is an artist who has never sold a painting. In fact, he had a career that has nothing to do with art. He was a colonel in the army. Bob doesn't look like an artist. He doesn't wear a quaint beret or paint-stained clothes. His face has no resemblance to a wild-eyed dreamer, such as the Dutch painter Van Gogh. No, Colonel Bob stands at attention, and he does everything precisely.

Ever since he retired from the army, Colonel Bob spends hours every day painting. Having been an officer affords, or gives, him the income to pursue his dream.

You may see Colonel Bob lurking and waiting for the right light, as though to surprise an enemy. He knows just when the sun should produce a glint, or shine, on a pond or a barn roof. He takes many pictures of a scene. Then he draws it on canvas and begins to paint. Nothing is simply green, blue, or yellow. One flower contains enough colors to fill two palettes. Colonel Bob says he sees everything with different eyes now.

 **Your Turn!**

 Need a Review?
For help with using context clues to determine the meanings of unfamiliar words, see page 117.

Ready to Try It?
As you read other text, use what you've learned about using context clues to help you determine the meanings of unfamiliar words.

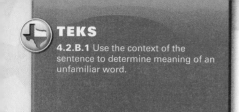

Envision It! Words to Know

abundance

backdrop

graze

ceremonial

drought

shock

READING STREET ONLINE
VOCABULARY ACTIVITIES
www.TexasReadingStreet.com

Vocabulary Strategy for

Unfamiliar Words

Context Clues Sometimes when you read, you come across a word you do not know. The context, or the words and sentences around the unknown word, may give you clues to the word's meaning.

1. Read the words and sentences around the unknown word. The author may have included a definition, synonym, or other clue to the word's meaning.

2. If not, say what the sentence means in your own words.

3. Think of a possible meaning for the unknown word.

4. Try that meaning in the sentence. Does it make sense?

As you read "Telling Stories," use context clues to help you figure out the meanings of *abundance* and *drought* and other unfamiliar words.

Words to Write Reread "Telling Stories." Think of a traditional story you have heard from someone in your family or a friend. Write a short summary of the story. Use words from the *Words to Know* list in your summary.

Telling Stories

Everyone tells stories. Sometimes we tell stories to shock each other. Sometimes we tell stories to calm ourselves before we go to bed. Often we tell stories to entertain each other. Before the written word, storytelling was much more than just entertainment. It was the way people passed down their traditions and their culture's history.

Many cultures that didn't have access to the written word used storytelling to make sense of their world. They would tell their stories around ceremonial campfires against the backdrop of the night sky. Sometimes they would use art. The Greeks told stories about the origins of their gods through images painted on pottery.

Stories also passed on morals, or lessons, that offer a culture's advice on how to behave. One popular Sioux story is about a last ear of corn that cries to a woman not to be left in the field. This story teaches not to waste food, whether in times of abundance or drought.

Because the stories were spoken, and passed from one generation to the next, sometimes the details of the stories changed. For example, in one version of a legend, the animals might graze on corn instead of grass. It all depended on the speaker's choice (and desire to make things interesting!). The important thing was to keep the lesson of the story and the tradition alive.

Your Turn!

 Need a Review?
For help with using context clues to determine the meanings of unfamiliar words, see page 117.

▶ **Ready to Try It?**
As you read other text, use what you've learned about using context clues to help you determine the meanings of unfamiliar words.

Antonyms

An antonym is a word that has the opposite meaning
of another word. *Day* is an antonym for *night*.

Day

Night

Antonym = Opposite

Strategy for Antonyms

1. Identify the word for which you want to
   find an antonym.
2. Think of other words or phrases that have
   the opposite meaning.
3. Use a thesaurus to help you find
   antonyms.
4. Use a dictionary to check the antonyms'
   meanings so that you use the word that
   best communicates your ideas.

Synonyms

A synonym is a word that has almost the same meaning as another word. *Hot* is a synonym for *scorching.*

Hot

Scorching

Synonym = Same

Strategy for Synonyms

1. Identify the word for which you want to find a synonym.
2. Think of other words or phrases that have the same, or almost the same, meaning.
3. Use a thesaurus to help you find more synonyms, and make a list.
4. Use a dictionary to find the word that best communicates your ideas.

TEKS
4.2.C.1 Complete analogies using knowledge of antonyms. 4.2.C.2 Complete analogies using knowledge of synonyms.

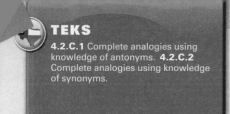

lassoed

prairie

riverbed

bargain

favor

offended

shrieked

Vocabulary Strategy for

🎯 Synonyms and Antonyms

Context Clues Synonyms and antonyms can be clues to the meaning of an unfamiliar word. Synonyms are words with almost the same meaning. In the analogy *boy* is to *man* as *girl* is to *woman, boy* and *man* are synonyms. Antonyms are words with opposite meanings. Use an antonym to complete this analogy: *girl* is to *boy* as *man* is to _____.

1. Complete this analogy using a word from the *Words to Know*: *laughed* is to *cried* as *whispered* is to _____.

2. Look at the sentence in which an unfamiliar word appears. The author may give a synonym or antonym in the same sentence.

3. If there is not a synonym or an antonym in the same sentence, check the sentences around it. If you find a synonym or an antonym, try it in the sentence.

As you read "Tall Paul," look for synonyms or antonyms to give you context clues to the meaning of any unfamiliar word.

Words to Write Imagine you met Tall Paul. Write a tale about Tall Paul and a day you spent with him. Use *Words to Know* in the tale.

Tall Paul

Tall Paul was a cowboy who lived on the plains not so long ago. He was not just any cowboy, though. He was so long-legged he could cross a mile of prairie in just one step. And he was so big and strong he lassoed and caught a whole herd of cattle with a single toss of his rope.

Tall Paul did not eat any small meals. No, he had a mighty big appetite. He ate a mountain of flapjacks for breakfast. One time, out on the range, he got so thirsty he drank a river. The dry riverbed just lay there gasping for water.

Tall Paul felt bad about that so he struck a bargain with the sky. The sky would bring a flood of rain. In return, the sky asked this favor: "I will help you if you do me this service. My servant, Wind, can't blow the clouds over that mountain there. I need you to flatten it a little for me."

Tall Paul said to the mountain, "Now don't be offended. I'll just take a little off the top." The mountain shrieked and screamed, but the deed was done. Tall Paul jumped on that mountain and turned it into a nice little mesa. In an instant, the rains began to fall.

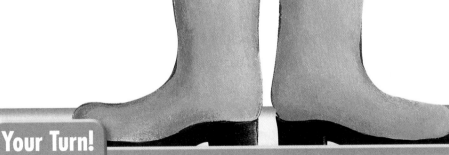

Your Turn!

⏸ Need a Review?
For additional help with synonyms and antonyms, see pages 126–127.

▶ Ready to Try It?
As you read other text, use what you've learned about synonyms and antonyms to help you understand it.

TEKS

4.2.B.1 Use the context of the sentence to determine meaning of an unfamiliar word. **4.2.C.1** Complete analogies using knowledge of antonyms.

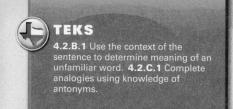

Envision It! | Words to Know

beakers

lecture

microscope

analysis

hollow

identity

precise

relentless

Vocabulary Strategy for

🎯 Synonyms and Antonyms

Context Clues Sometimes an author will use a synonym or an antonym as a clue to help you determine the meaning of a word. Synonyms are words that have almost the same meaning. Antonyms are words with opposite meanings.

1. Think about synonyms and antonyms to complete this analogy using one of the vocabulary words from *Words to Know: excited* is to *calm* as *solid* is to _____.

2. When you read a word you don't know, reread the sentence with the unfamiliar word. Read the words and sentences around it. Look for a synonym or an antonym.

3. If you find a synonym or an antonym, try using it in place of the unfamiliar word. Does the synonym or antonym help you or clarify the meaning of the unfamiliar word?

As you read "A Scientist's Journal," check the context of words you don't know. Look for a synonym or an antonym to help you figure out an unfamiliar word.

Words to Write Reread "A Scientist's Journal." Imagine that you are writing in your journal about an experiment you performed. Use words from the *Words to Know* list.

A Scientist's Journal

Day 1. I'm about ready to perform my experiment. After listening to Professor Wilson's lecture, I got inspired. His speech made me eager and excited about testing a theory I have about some seeds.

Day 2. Yesterday, I examined the seeds in question with my microscope. I looked at the seeds up close and saw that none of them had decayed; instead, they all seemed to be healthy.

Day 3. I emptied the beakers of seeds into a pan. I have made sure my measurements of the pan were not just a guess but that they were very precise. I rechecked my theory so I could give it my final analysis before completing the experiment tomorrow.

Day 4. I am relentless; I won't give up. I put a lid on the pan and began to heat the seeds on the warming device. Soon, a crackling noise began inside the pan. Then it reached a peak and suddenly stopped. I tapped the pan. It once sounded empty and hollow, but it now sounded full. I opened the lid and proved my theory. The seeds were popcorn seeds! I like my new identity as a scientist—being a scientist can be delicious!

Your Turn!

❚❚ Need a Review?
For additional help with synonyms and antonyms, see pages 126–127.

▶ Ready to Try It?
As you read other text, use what you've learned about synonyms and antonyms to help you understand it.

TEKS

4.2.B.1 Use the context of the sentence to determine meaning of an unfamiliar word. **4.2.C.1** Complete analogies using knowledge of antonyms and synonyms.

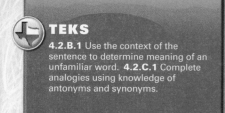

Envision It! | Words to Know

lizards

reptiles

salamanders

amphibians

crime

exhibit

reference

stumped

Vocabulary Strategy for

Synonyms and Antonyms

Context Clues You can use the context of a sentence to help determine the meaning of an unfamiliar word. The clue may be a synonym or an antonym. Synonyms are words that have the same meaning. Antonyms have the opposite meanings.

1. Complete this analogy using a word from the *Words to Know* and your knowledge of synonyms and antonyms: *big* is to *large* as *confused* is to _____.

2. Reread the sentence with the unfamiliar word. Look for a synonym or an antonym. Does the synonym make sense in the sentence? Does the antonym help you figure out the unfamiliar word's definition?

3. If there is not a synonym or an antonym in the same sentence, check the sentences around it. If you find a synonym or an antonym there, try it in the sentence.

As you read "It Is Not All in the Family," use context clues or synonyms and antonyms to help you figure out any unfamiliar words.

Words to Write Reread "It Is Not All in the Family." Imagine you are a zoo worker who will explain the differences between reptiles and amphibians. Write the points that you will make about each. Use words from *Words to Know*.

IT IS NOT ALL IN THE FAMILY

Are you interested in the world of snakes, frogs, turtles, lizards, toads, and salamanders? You probably think of all of these animals as one big creepy family. In fact, they are not. Snakes, turtles, and lizards are all reptiles. Frogs, toads, and salamanders are all amphibians. Do you know the differences between these types of animals? If you are stumped, read on.

Amphibians have skin that must be kept wet. If you touch the skin, it feels slimy. This is because amphibians live near water. They lay their eggs in water because the eggs have no shell. Reptiles, on the other hand, have dry skin that is covered with scales. Their eggs have a tough covering. These eggs can be laid on land.

If you are still baffled or confused about these animals, read about them in a reference book, such as an encyclopedia. The next time you are at a zoo, look them up. A zoo exhibit has live animals that you can see up close. The display gives facts about the animals. Remember, it is not a crime to ask questions! Zoo workers like to share what they know.

Your Turn!

 Need a Review?
For additional help with synonyms and antonyms, see pages 126–127.

 Ready to Try It?
As you read other text, use what you've learned about synonyms and antonyms to help you understand it.

TEKS

4.2.B.1 Use the context of the sentence to determine meaning of an unfamiliar word. **4.2.C.2** Complete analogies using knowledge of synonyms.

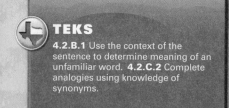

Envision It! Words to Know

rille

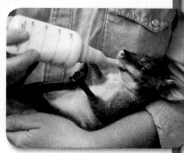

runt

trench

loomed

staggered

summoning

taunted

trudged

READING STREET ONLINE
VOCABULARY ACTIVITIES
www.TexasReadingStreet.com

Vocabulary Strategy for

Synonyms

Context Clues Sometimes a synonym can be a clue to help you figure out the meaning of a word. Look at the sentence: *The tiny spider was so miniscule I almost stepped on it.* You can use the synonym *tiny* to help you figure out the meaning of *miniscule*.

1. Use what you know about synonyms to complete this analogy with a word from *Words to Know: marched* is to *hiked* as *tramped* is to _____.

2. When you read a word you don't know, read the words and sentences around it. Look for a synonym.

3. If you find a synonym, try using it in place of the unfamiliar word. Then see if it makes sense.

As you read "Gone to the Moon," check the context of words you don't know. Look for a synonym to help you figure out the unfamiliar word.

Words to Write Reread "Gone to the Moon." Imagine that you are the first fourth grader to travel to the moon. Your job is to send back messages describing what you see and how you feel as you walk on the moon. Use words from the *Words to Know* list in your message.

Gone to the Moon

People have long dreamed of going to the moon. Maybe this is because the moon circles so close by. No other thing in space is closer to Earth. How could we not conquer this small thing, this runt?

When the machine age arrived, the moon still taunted us. "I'm so close," it teased. "Why don't you come on up?" In 1969, three people did. Summoning all our knowledge and technology, we sent them into space and guided them to the moon. They had to call on all their bravery to blast off into the unknown.

Imagine how their hearts raced as the moon loomed before them. Imagine their awe as two of them stepped where no person had ever set foot. They saw craters and a rille, a narrow valley that looks like a trench.

With every step, they leaped rather than trudged. (On Earth, because of gravity, we plod along.) It was easy to pick up moon rocks under whose weight they would have staggered and stumbled on Earth.

Was it worth it to go to the moon? Yes!

 **Your Turn!**

 Need a Review?
For additional help with synonyms, see page 127.

▷ **Ready to Try It?**
As you read other text, use what you've learned about synonyms to help you understand it.

Prefixes

A prefix is a word part added to the beginning of a base word to form a new word.

Wrap

Unwrap

Common Prefixes and Their Meanings

un-	not
re-	again, back
in-	not
dis-	not, opposite of
pre-	before

Strategy for Prefixes

1. Look at the unknown word and identify the prefix.
2. What does the base word mean? If you're not sure, check a dictionary.
3. Use what you know about the base word and the prefix to figure out the meaning of the unknown word.
4. Use a dictionary to check your guess.

Suffixes

A suffix is a word part added to the end of
a base word to form a new word.

Shoeless

Shoe

Common Suffixes and Their Meanings

-ly	characteristic of
-tion	act, process
-able	can be done
-ment	action or process
-less	without

Strategy for Suffixes

1. Look at the unknown word and identify the suffix.
2. What does the base word mean? If you're not sure, check a dictionary.
3. Use what you know about the base word and the suffix to figure out the meaning of the unknown word.
4. Use a dictionary to check your guess.

TEKS

4.2.A.6 Determine meaning of grade-level academic English words derived from other linguistic affixes.

memorial

prideful

selecting

grand

peculiar

positive

recalls

Vocabulary Strategy for

Affixes: Suffixes

Word Structure Suppose you read an academic vocabulary word you don't know. You can use the suffix to help you figure out the word's meaning. Does the word have *-ful* or *-al* at the end? The Old English suffix *-ful* can make a word mean "full of," as in *tasteful*. The Old English suffix *-al* can make a word mean "of or like," as in *magical*.

1. Put your finger over the *-ful* or *-al* suffix.

2. Look at the base word, the part of the word without the suffix. Put the base word in the phrase "full of _____" or "of or like _____."

3. Try that meaning in the sentence. Does it make sense?

As you read "The Storyteller," look for words that end in *-ful* or *-al*. Use the suffixes to help you figure out the meanings of academic vocabulary words.

Words to Write Reread "The Storyteller." Write a short essay about what you like best about the library. Use words from the *Words to Know* list in your essay.

The Storyteller

Thursday mornings at the James P. Guthrie Memorial Library are magical. That's because every Thursday morning Ms. Ada Landry tells historical fiction stories to anyone who wants to listen. But she does not just tell the stories. She acts them out. She makes them come alive.

When Ms. Ada describes what she calls "a prideful person," she puffs out her chest and looks down her nose. She talks in a loud, boastful, powerful voice. When she tells about a sly person, she narrows her eyes and pulls up her shoulders. She talks in a shady kind of voice. When she recalls things that happened long ago, she gets a faraway look in her eyes, and she talks in a quiet, dreamy, hopeful voice.

Ms. Ada's stories are entertaining, but they nearly always have a lesson in them too. A person who everyone thinks is a bit peculiar turns out to be kind or brave. A person who everyone thinks is grand proves to be cowardly or mean. A mistake or disaster ends up having a positive effect.

When it comes to selecting and telling stories, Ms. Ada is the best.

Your Turn!

Need a Review?
For additional help with suffixes, see page 137.

Ready to Try It?
As you read other text, use what you've learned about suffixes to help you understand it.

TEKS

4.2.A.3 Determine meaning of grade-level academic English words derived from other linguistic roots.

Envision It! Words to Know

glacier

slopes

wilderness

impressive

naturalist

preserve

species

READING STREET ONLINE
VOCABULARY ACTIVITIES
www.TexasReadingStreet.com

Vocabulary Strategy for

Affixes: Suffixes -*ist*, -*ive*, -*ness*

Word Structure Suppose you come to an academic word that has the suffix -*ist*, -*ive*, or -*ness* at the end. You can use the suffix to figure out the word's meaning. The Latin suffix -*ist* makes a word mean "one who is an expert," as in *biologist*, an expert in biology. The Greek suffix -*ive* can make a word mean "tending or inclined to" as in *active*, which means "tending to act." The Old English -*ness* means "the quality of," as in *goodness*.

1. Find a word with the suffix -*ist*, -*ive*, or -*ness*. Put your finger over the suffix.

2. Look at the base word. Put the base word in the phrase "one who is an expert in ____" or "tending or inclined to ____" or "the quality of ____."

3. Does that meaning make sense in the sentence?

Use what you know about suffixes to figure out academic vocabulary as you read "Letter from Denali."

Words to Write Reread "Letter from Denali." Think of a park or other natural setting that you have seen. Write a letter to a friend describing it. Use words from the *Words to Know* list.

Letter from Denali

Dear Kevin,

We are in Denali National Park in Alaska. Denali is a gigantic park. The emptiness is overwhelming. It has more than six million acres of wilderness, so we certainly won't be seeing the whole park!

Denali was established to preserve the land, the animals, and plants that live here. More than 650 species of flowering plants and 217 species of animals live in Denali! That's what the naturalist on the guided walk told us yesterday. Our group was very attentive when a botanist who was with us said that to live in Denali year-round, a plant or animal species has to be able to survive long, cold winters.

Today we hiked up the slopes of Mt. McKinley. It is the highest mountain in North America, and it is part of Denali. We could see a giant glacier looking like a huge field of ice farther up on the mountain. It was a very impressive sight. Mt. McKinley has several glaciers, and some are more than 30 miles long!

I have taken a zillion pictures, but I really think this is a place you have to see in person.

Love,

Lisa

Your Turn!

❚❚ Need a Review?
For additional help with suffixes, see page 137.

▶ Ready to Try It?
As you read other text, use what you've learned about suffixes to help you understand it.

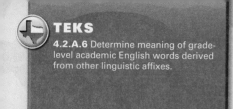

TEKS

4.2.A.6 Determine meaning of grade-level academic English words derived from other linguistic affixes.

Envision It! | Words to Know

hoop

jersey

rim

fouled

marveled

speechless

swatted

unbelievable

Vocabulary Strategy for

🎯 Affixes: Prefixes and Suffixes

Word Structure Prefixes and suffixes have their own meanings. When they are added to words, they change the meaning of the original word, or the base word. The Middle English prefix *un-* means "the opposite of " or "not," as in *undefeated.* The suffix *-able* means "able to be," as in *unbeatable.* The Middle English suffix *-less* means "without," as in *scoreless.* You can use affixes to help you figure out the meanings of words.

1. Look at an unfamiliar word to see if it has a base word you know.

2. Has the prefix *un-* or the suffix *-able* or *-less* been added to the base word?

3. Think about how the prefix or suffix changes the meaning of the base word.

4. Try the meaning in the sentence to see if it makes sense.

Read "At the Game." Look for prefixes and suffixes to help you figure out the meanings of unfamiliar words.

Words to Write Reread "At the Game." Imagine that you just played a game of basketball. Write a paragraph describing the game. Use words from the *Words to Know* list.

At the Game

"Hello again, sports fans. This is Bud Sherman, WXXT Channel 6, coming to you from the Grandview Center, where the third-place Tigers are battling the second-place Lions in the first round of the HSBA playoffs. Tiger forward Matt Roberts has had a flawless game, scoring 28 points so far. Lion center Darren Jones has been unbelievable under the basket.

"Now Roberts moves in and shoots the ball. He's looking for another three-pointer. The ball hits the rim. Maxwell tries a shot, but it's swatted away by Jones.

Grundig has the ball and he's heading for the Tigers' hoop. Oh, my, he's been fouled by Lee, who grabbed Grundig's jersey and arm. I imagine Coach Simmons is unhappy. That's Lee's fourth foul in this half. Grundig, a reliable free-thrower, makes both points. Pfizer throws in to Barton, who passes to—Roberts!

"You know, I have always marveled at the way Roberts moves around the court, but his performance tonight just leaves me speechless. Roberts shoots from 30 feet out, and he scores! The Tigers win, 87-84."

Your Turn!

 **Need a Review?**
For additional help with prefixes and suffixes, see pages 136–137.

Ready to Try It?
As you read other text, use what you've learned about prefixes and suffixes to help you understand it.

TEKS

4.2.A.6 Determine meaning of grade-level academic English words derived from other linguistic affixes.

Envision It! | Words to Know

argument

descendants

script

advice

arrangements

dishonest

snag

READING STREET ONLINE
VOCABULARY ACTIVITIES
www.TexasReadingStreet.com

Vocabulary Strategy for

Affixes: Prefixes

Word Structure Prefixes are word parts that are added to the beginning of words. A prefix changes a word's meaning. For example, the Middle English prefix *dis-* means "not." If you *disagree*, you do not agree with someone or something. Knowing what a prefix means can help you figure out the meaning of an unknown word as you read.

1. Find a sentence with a word that has a prefix. Cover the prefix with your finger.

2. Look at the base word. See if you know what it means.

3. Add the meaning of the prefix.

4. Check to see if this meaning makes sense in the sentence.

Read "Writing a Play About History." Use prefixes to help you determine the meanings of words you do not know.

Words to Write Reread "Writing a Play About History." Write a paragraph about a historical event you would like to see performed as a play. Use words from the *Words to Know* list in your paragraph.

Writing a Play About History

If you decide to write a play about history, make arrangements to spend time on research. Sometimes there is some argument about which facts are true. Although few writers mean to be dishonest, they may not always check their facts. Be a little distrustful of what you read.

It might be interesting to write about the descendants of those who sailed on the *Mayflower*. Some of our Presidents, including Presidents John Adams, John Quincy Adams, and Franklin Roosevelt, had ancestors on the *Mayflower*. Astronaut Alan Shepard Jr. is also part of this special group. I'm sure you'll be able to discover more names to add to this list!

Your work can hit a snag if you don't make your information interesting. Take this advice and make sure your script tells a good story. You'll learn a lot while writing your play. You'll want to work hard to make sure your audience enjoys every minute!

Your Turn!

 Need a Review?
For additional help with prefixes, see page 136.

 Ready to Try It?
As you read other text, use what you've learned about prefixes to help you understand it.

TEKS

4.2.A.6 Determine meaning of grade-level academic English words derived from other linguistic affixes.

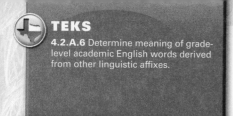

Envision It! | Words to Know

harness

lumberjacks

thaw

announcement

feature

requirements

unnatural

untamed

Vocabulary Strategy for

⟳ Affixes: Suffixes

Word Structure A suffix is a word part that is added to the end of a word. When a suffix is added to a base word, it changes the meaning of the word. For example, the Middle English base word of *boldly* is *bold*, which means "fearless" or "courageous." The suffix *-ly* means "having the form or appearance of." So, *boldly* means "appearing courageous."

1. Look at the unknown word to see if it has a base word that you know.

2. Check to see if a suffix has been added to the base word.

3. Ask yourself how the suffix changes the meaning of the base word.

4. Try that meaning in the sentence to see if it makes sense.

Use what you know about suffixes to figure out the meanings of *announcement, requirements, unnatural,* and other unknown words as you read "Working with Babe."

Words to Write Reread "Working with Babe." Write a paragraph about a time when you worked hard. How did you feel when you finished? Use words from the *Words to Know* list in your writing.

Working with Babe

Back in the old days, lumberjacks used oxen to help move logs out of the woods. At first, when Paul Bunyan opened his own logging camp, Babe the Blue Ox did all the work himself. Paul's camp was so successful that Babe soon needed help. At the start of the spring thaw, he put up an announcement calling for oxen to help him.

Besides the obvious feature of being huge, Babe asked that the oxen that applied be

- strong enough to pull logs 300 feet in diameter,
- wide enough to hold a 10-foot basket of food on their backs,
- tame enough to care for a newborn lamb.

Babe did not have time to deal with untamed oxen. He needed them to be able to go right to work. Hundreds of oxen showed up to work. Before being hired, the oxen boldly said they had some requirements of their own. They each wanted ten bags of oats a day. They each wanted a harness lined with the softest fur. And, even though it seemed unnatural, they wanted an endless supply of chocolate chips! It is a well-kept secret that oxen love sweets.

Your Turn!

 Need a Review?
For additional help with suffixes, see page 137.

 Ready to Try It?
As you read other text, use what you've learned about suffixes to help you understand it.

TEKS

4.2.A.4 Determine meaning of grade-level academic English words derived from Latin affixes. **4.2.A.5** Determine meaning of grade-level academic English words derived from Greek affixes.

Envision It! Words to Know

continent

depart

TO ALL TRAINS

icebergs

anticipation

convergence

forbidding

heaves

**READING STREET ONLINE
VOCABULARY ACTIVITIES**
www.TexasReadingStreet.com

Vocabulary Strategy for

Greek and Latin Prefixes

Word Structure Many English academic vocabulary words have Latin or Greek prefixes. The Latin prefix *de-* means "away from" and appears in words such as *defrost*. The prefix *con-* means "with" or "together," as in *connect*. The Greek prefix *geo-* means "of the earth's surface" and *pan-* means "all." You can use what you know about prefixes to help you figure out the meaning of an unknown word.

1. Look at the unknown word. Does it have a Latin or Greek prefix that you know?

2. Think about whether or not the prefix affects the meaning of the unknown word.

3. Try the meaning in the sentence to be sure it makes sense.

As you read "The Hunger to Know," use what you know about Greek and Latin prefixes to figure out the meanings of *depart, continent, geography, panorama,* and other academic words.

Words to Write Reread "The Hunger to Know." Imagine that you are part of a team that has spent two years exploring space. You've returned to Earth and are talking to reporters about your trip. Someone asks, "What made you decide to travel to space?" Use words from the *Words to Know* list in your answer.

THE HUNGER TO KNOW

There is something in us that yearns to explore new places. Often these places are dangerous, even forbidding. That doesn't stop us from going there, though. In fact, risk may be part of what calls to us.

Five hundred years ago, the continent of North America lay waiting. Explorers from Europe sailed the Atlantic. Filled with anticipation, they couldn't wait to depart. These adventurers had no idea what the geography of this new land would be. Would they find treasure or be killed by monsters? They were ready for the new, the strange, the unexpected.

Today men and women still wonder, plan, and go. They travel to the ocean floor. There they see fantastic forms of life. They view wild panorama of mountains and canyons formed when the stuff of Earth heaves and twists. They sail through fields of icebergs to the frozen poles. They blast into space, leaving the only home humans have ever known.

What drives people so? It may be the convergence of two needs: the hunger to know and the desire to be the first. Whatever makes it so, we gain from it. As long as we keep seeking and learning, our world keeps growing.

Your Turn!

‖ Need a Review?
For additional help with prefixes, see page 136.

 Ready to Try It?
As you read other text, use what you've learned about Greek and Latin prefixes to help you understand it.

Dictionary

A dictionary is a reference book that lists words alphabetically. It can be used to look up definitions, parts of speech, spelling, and other forms of words.

punc•tu•al ❶ (pungk′ chü əl), ❷ ADJECTIVE. ❸ prompt; exactly on time: ❹ *He is always punctual.* ❺ ✹ ADVERB **punc′tu•al•ly.**

❶ Pronunciation

❷ Part of speech

❸ Definitions

❹ Example sentence

❺ Other form of the word and its part of speech

Strategy for Dictionary

1. Identify the unknown word.
2. Look up the word in a dictionary. Entries are listed alphabetically.
3. Find the part of the entry that has the information you are looking for.
4. Use the diagram above as a guide to help you locate the information you want.

Thesaurus

A thesaurus is a book of synonyms. Sometimes it will also contain antonyms. Look through the synonyms to find one with the best meaning by using a dictionary.

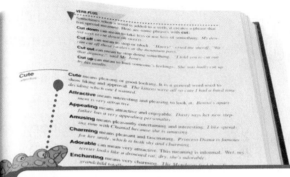

cute
adjective
attractive, appealing, amusing, charming, adorable, enchanting.
ANTONYMS: ugly, dull, unappealing

Strategy for Thesaurus

1. Look up the word in a thesaurus. Entries are listed alphabetically.
2. Locate the synonyms for your word.
3. Find the word with the exact meaning you want.

TEKS

4.2.E.1 Use a dictionary or glossary to determine meanings of unknown words. **4.2.E.2** Use a dictionary or glossary to determine syllabication of unknown words. **4.2.E.3** Use a dictionary or glossary to determine pronunciation of unknown words.

Envision It! | Words to Know

coyote

roundup

spurs

bawling

dudes

Vocabulary Strategy for

🔊 Unknown Words

Dictionary/Glossary When you read, you may come across a word you don't know. If the author has not given any context clues in the words and sentences around the word, then you can use a dictionary or glossary to figure out the word's meaning.

1. Check the back of your book for a glossary. If there is no glossary, look up the word in a dictionary.

2. Find the entry for the word. The entries are listed in alphabetical order.

3. Each word is divided into syllables. Use the syllabication to help you pronounce the word. If you are still having difficulty, use the pronunciation key.

4. Read all the meanings given for the word.

5. Choose the meaning that makes sense in the sentence.

Use a dictionary or the glossary to help you determine the meanings, pronunciations, and syllabication of unknown words as you read " At a Guest Ranch."

Words to Write Reread "At a Guest Ranch." Imagine that you are staying at a dude ranch. Write a journal entry describing a day at the ranch. Use words from the *Words to Know* list in your journal entry.

AT A GUEST RANCH

Howdy, partner! That may sound corny, but it's appropriate because my family and I are at a ranch that lets people pay to stay here and see what ranch life is like. Guests are called dudes. That's what the cowhands called people from back East. Some dude ranches are just for entertaining visitors, excuse me, dudes. Some are real cattle or sheep ranches that take in a few dudes on the side.

Our ranch, the Double K near Bozeman, Montana, is a working cattle ranch. Yesterday we went with the cowhands on a roundup. It was exciting to watch. With just a touch of his spurs, a cowhand moved his horse into the herd and cut out one cow. It was hot, dusty, and noisy too. The cattle were mooing, and the calves were bawling.

We also rode out on a trail and camped out under the stars. Dinner from a chuckwagon, a bedroll by the campfire, and a coyote howling in the distance — I felt as if I were in a Western movie!

Your Turn!

 Need a Review?
For help with using a dictionary to determine the meanings of unknown words, see page 150.

 Ready to Try It?
As you read other text, use what you've learned about using a dictionary or glossary to help you find the meanings of unknown words.

TEKS

4.2.E.1 Use a dictionary or glossary to determine meanings of unknown words. **4.2.E.2** Use a dictionary or glossary to determine syllabication of unknown words. **4.2.E.3** Use a dictionary or glossary to determine pronunciation of unknown words.

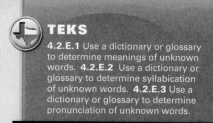

Envision It! | Words to Know

infested

landslide

roamed

ambition

quicksand

resistance

rickety

vast

READING STREET ONLINE
VOCABULARY ACTIVITIES
www.TexasReadingStreet.com

Vocabulary Strategy for

Unknown Words

Dictionary/Glossary When you are reading, you may come across a word you don't know. If you can't use the context, or words and sentences around the unknown word, to figure out its meaning, you can use a dictionary or glossary for help.

1. Look in the back of your book for the glossary.

2. Find the entry for the word. The entries are in alphabetical order.

3. Use the pronunciation key to pronounce the word. Do you see how the word is broken into syllables?

4. Read all the meanings given for the word.

5. Choose the meaning that makes the best sense in the sentence.

Read "Racing Dreams." Use the glossary to help you figure out the meanings, syllabications, and pronunciations of this week's *Words to Know*.

Words to Write Reread "Racing Dreams." Imagine that you're a reporter at a horse race. Write a news article on the race. Use words from the *Words to Know* list in your article.

154

RACING Dreams

One summer my parents sent me to camp in Wisconsin. I spent a lot of time taking horseback-riding lessons. It was my ambition to become a great rider. As we roamed down the trails, I dreamed about being a famous rider.

First, my imaginary horse and I would gallop over the vast plains. We would leap over rickety gates and pass untouched through fields infested with locusts. My horse would amaze everyone with his bravery. He would leap over quicksand without the slightest resistance. My horse would be so fast that he could outrun a landslide. Nothing would scare him!

Everyone would want us to run in a great race. My horse and I would train for long hours. We would work hard. The day would come, and all the fastest horses and their riders would be there to see who was the best. My horse and I would fly around the track. We would pass all the other horses.

Your Turn!

⏸ Need a Review?
For help with using a dictionary to determine the meanings of unknown words, see page 150.

▶ Ready to Try It?
As you read other text, use what you've learned about using a dictionary or glossary to help you find the meanings of unknown words.

TEKS
4.2.E.1 Use a dictionary or glossary to determine meanings of unknown words. **4.2.E.2** Use a dictionary or glossary to determine syllabication of unknown words. **4.2.E.3** Use a dictionary or glossary to determine pronunciation of unknown words.

Envision It! | Words to Know

Constitution

howling

politics

SMITH for DENT

humble

responsibility

solemnly

vain

READING STREET ONLINE
VOCABULARY ACTIVITIES
www.TexasReadingStreet.com

Vocabulary Strategy for

Unknown Words

Dictionary/Glossary When you are reading, you may come across a word you don't know. If you can't use the context, or words and sentences around the word, to figure out the word's meaning, you can use a dictionary or glossary to help you.

1. Check the back of your book for a glossary. If there is no glossary, look up the word in a dictionary.

2. Find the entry for the word. The entries are in alphabetical order.

3. To yourself, say the word broken into syllables or use the pronunciation key to help you pronounce the word. Saying the word may help you recognize it.

4. Read all the meanings given for the word.

5. Choose the meaning that makes sense in the sentence.

Read "Class Election." Use context clues, a dictionary, or the glossary to help you determine the meanings, syllabications, and pronunciations of this week's *Words to Know.*

Words to Write Reread "Class Election." Imagine that you have just been elected class president. Now you need to write your acceptance speech. Use words from the *Words to Know* list in your speech.

Class Election

The students in Grade 4 are electing class officers. Four students are running for president.

Steven is vain about his looks. He puts just his name and his face on his signs. He says politics is dull, but winning is fun. Suzanne acts humble about how well she plays sports. Yet all her signs show her making the winning goal in last year's soccer championship. Omar solemnly promises that he will run a clean campaign. Then he makes fun of the other candidates. Still, his speeches are a howling success. Maya says that unlike the President of the United States, the president of Grade 4 does not have to "protect and defend the Constitution of the United States." However, she says the Grade 4 president does have a responsibility to all the students in Grade 4, not just the ones who voted for him or her. Maya was Grade 3 president and is captain of the softball team. If you were a student in Grade 4, whom would you vote for?

Your Turn!

❚❚ Need a Review?
For help with using a dictionary to determine the meanings of unknown words, see page 150.

▶ Ready to Try It?
As you read other text, use what you've learned about using a dictionary or glossary to help you find the meanings of unknown words.

TEKS

4.2.E.1 Use a dictionary or glossary to determine meanings of unknown words. **4.2.E.3** Use a dictionary or glossary to determine pronunciation of unknown words.

Envision It! | Words to Know

exhausting

intense

messages

advance

developed

impossible

headquarters

reveal

READING STREET ONLINE
VOCABULARY ACTIVITIES
www.TexasReadingStreet.com

Vocabulary Strategy for

🔁 Unknown Words

Dictionary/Glossary When you read, you may come across a word you don't know. If you can't use the context, or words and sentences around the unknown word, to figure it out, you can use a dictionary or a glossary to help you.

1. Look in the back of your book for the glossary.

2. Find the entry for the word. The entries are in alphabetical order.

3. Use the pronunciation key to pronounce the word.

4. Read all the meanings given for the word.

5. Choose the meaning that makes the best sense in the sentence.

As you read "A New Way to Win a War," use context clues to figure out the meanings of this week's *Words to Know*. If the context doesn't help, use a dictionary or the glossary to determine their meanings.

Words to Write Reread "A New Way to Win a War." Imagine you were in a place where no one spoke your language. Write about how you could try to communicate with another person. Use some of the *Words to Know* in your writing.

A New Way to Win A War

During World War II, a group of marines known as Navajo code talkers developed a special code to send and receive secret messages. A different Navajo word stood for each letter of the English alphabet. The code was impossible for the Japanese to figure out. It was based on the Navajo language, which is very difficult to learn.

To help advance the United States troops and their allies, code talkers were often in the areas with the most intense fighting. The code talkers would reveal the location of the enemy during battle and send the coded message back to headquarters. Knowing this information, the United States and its allies were able to determine what to do next. Fighting during the war was exhausting, and the radios and equipment the code talkers had to carry made it even more difficult.

But because of their hard work and sacrifice, Navajo code talkers helped the U.S. to victory in World War II.

Your Turn!

❚❚ Need a Review?
For help with using a dictionary to determine the meanings of unknown words, see page 150.

▶ Ready to Try It?
As you read other text, use what you've learned about using a dictionary or glossary to help you find the meanings of unknown words.

Multiple-Meaning Words

Multiple-meaning words are words that have different meanings depending on how they are used. Homonyms, homographs, and homophones are all multiple-meaning words.

Homographs

Homographs are words that are spelled the same but have different meanings and sometimes different pronunciations.

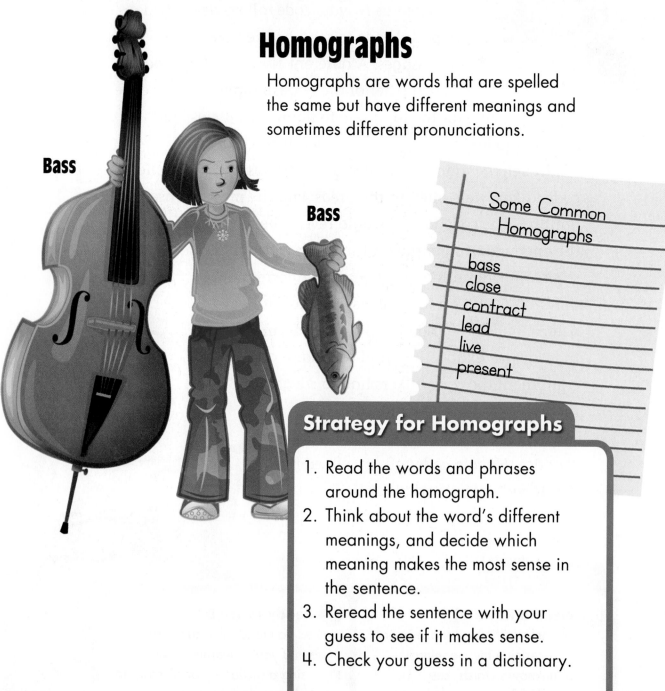

Bass

Bass

Some Common Homographs

bass
close
contract
lead
live
present

Strategy for Homographs

1. Read the words and phrases around the homograph.
2. Think about the word's different meanings, and decide which meaning makes the most sense in the sentence.
3. Reread the sentence with your guess to see if it makes sense.
4. Check your guess in a dictionary.

Homonyms

Homonyms are words that are pronounced the same and have the same spelling, but their meanings are different.

Squash

Squash

Strategy for Homonyms

1. Read the words and phrases near the homonym.
2. Think about the word's different meanings, and decide which one makes the most sense.
3. Reread the sentence with your guess to see if it makes sense.
4. Use a dictionary to check your guess.

Some Common Homonyms

pen
duck
ear
bank
bark

Homophones

Homophones are words that are pronounced the same way but have different spellings and different meanings.

Ball

Bawl

Some Common
Homophones

ate	eight
bored	board
brake	break
knight	night
weight	wait

Strategy for Homophones

1. Think about the different spellings and meanings of the homophone.
2. Check a dictionary for definitions of the words.
3. Use the word that best fits your writing.

This chart can help you remember the differences between homonyms, homographs, and homophones.

Understanding Homographs, Homonyms, and Homophones

	Pronunciation	Spelling	Meaning
Homographs	may be the same or different	same	different
Homonyms	same	same	different
Homophones	same	different	different

Homograph

present

present

bark

Homonym

bark

aisle

Homophone

isle

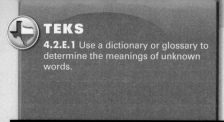

Envision It! | Words to Know

badger

jointed

rushes

bank
bristled
patched
ruffled

READING STREET ONLINE
VOCABULARY ACTIVITIES
www.TexasReadingStreet.com

Vocabulary Strategy for

Multiple-Meaning Words

Dictionary/Glossary You may read a word whose meaning you know, but the word doesn't make sense in the sentence. The word may have more than one meaning, or multiple meanings. Use a dictionary or glossary to find the meaning that fits.

1. Try the meaning that you know. Does it make sense in the sentence?

2. If it doesn't, look up the word to see what other meanings it has.

3. Read all the meanings given for the word. Try each meaning in the sentence.

4. Choose the one that makes the most sense.

Read "Foggy River Schoolhouse." Stop at any words that have multiple meanings, such as *bank* or *ruffled*. Look them up in a dictionary or glossary to see what other meanings they could have.

Words to Write Reread "Foggy River Schoolhouse." Imagine that you live in the nineteenth century and go to school in a one-room schoolhouse. Write a journal entry describing a typical day. Use words from the *Words to Know* list.

FOGGY RIVER SCHOOLHOUSE

My older brother, Edward, got me in trouble today. He wanted to make me laugh, so he threw sticky burrs at me during Miss Osgood's arithmetic lesson. Some of the burrs landed on my desk and were easy to throw right back at Edward, but a few of those bristled burrs got caught in the folds of my ruffled petticoat. I had such trouble getting them unstuck from the cloth that Edward couldn't hold in his laughter. Miss Osgood was not happy and she sent both of us to the corner to face the wall.

My teacher, Miss Osgood, calls me a "country girl" because I'd rather play outside in the rushes than sit inside and learn arithmetic. Who would blame me! That schoolroom can get pretty cramped. All of the students from Foggy River learn in the same room. I do love to practice drawing the jointed letters of the alphabet, but I'd much rather do it on the soft bank of the open creek where I might catch a glimpse of a badger or a beaver.

Maybe when I get older I'll like being at school more. Then I'll be able to chop wood for the stove and fetch water, which means I'll get to go outside! Edward is older, so he gets to do these chores. My school chore is to clap the erasers.

Even at home, my chores keep me inside. Tonight I have to mend the hole in Edward's patched flannel shirt. Maybe I'll choose a mismatched color for his patch!

Your Turn!

⏸ Need a Review?
For additional help with multiple-meaning words, see pages 160–163.

▶ Ready to Try It?
As you read other text, use what you've learned about multiple-meaning words to help you understand it.

TEKS

4.2.B.2 Use the context of the sentence to determine meaning of multiple meaning words.

Envision It! | Words to Know

atmosphere

chemical

scales

apprentice

club

essay

manufacturing

pressure

Vocabulary Strategy for

Multiple-Meaning Words

Context Clues When you read you might see a word whose meaning you know, but the word doesn't make sense in the sentence. The word may have more than one meaning. You can look for clues, such as an example or definition, in the text to help you decide which meaning the author is using.

1. First, try the meaning you know. Does it make sense in the sentence?

2. If that meaning doesn't make sense, reread the words and sentences around the word. Use context clues to try to figure out a meaning for the word.

3. Try that meaning in the sentence to see if it makes sense.

Read "And the Winner Is. . . ." Use context clues to help you figure out the meanings of this week's *Words to Know* and multiple-meaning words.

Words to Write Reread "And the Winner Is . . . ." Imagine that you are a TV meteorologist. Write your script for tonight's weathercast. Use words from the *Words to Know* list.

And the Winner Is . . .

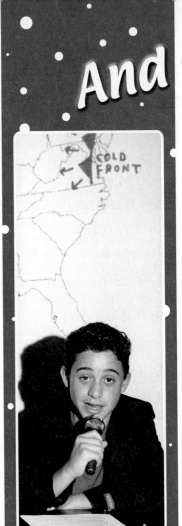

Rob's twin, Jill, ran into the family room where Rob and his friend Ryan were working on homework. Waving an envelope, she yelled, "Rob! It's from the Forecaster Club; the club you wanted to join! Do you think it's about the essay you wrote? You know, the one about using pine-cone scales to predict weather?"

Rob ripped the letter out of the envelope. "Yes! My essay won! I'm going to be a meteorologist's apprentice for a day! Remember I told you that some scientists have been manufacturing a new weather detector? Well, I'll be one of the first people to watch them use it!"

Ryan was the one who told Rob about the contest. He knew how crazy his friend was about forecasting the weather, so he really put the pressure on Rob to enter. Ryan was thrilled when Rob won, even though he knew he'd have to put up with Rob's constant weather updates! Just then, Rob announced, "A severe cold front will be moving across our region later today, so get out your winter jackets! The chemical composition of the gases in the air will change significantly as the day goes on...."

Suddenly the room's atmosphere changed, as Ryan groaned jokingly and muttered to Jill, "At least we'll know what clothes to wear—every single minute of the day!"

Your Turn!

 Need a Review?
For additional help with multiple-meaning words, see pages 160–163.

▶ **Ready to Try It?**
As you read other text, use what you've learned about multiple-meaning words to help you understand it.

TEKS
4.2.B.2 Use the context of the
sentence to determine meaning of
multiple meaning words.

bluff

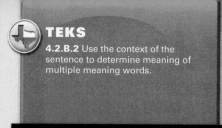

lagoon

tropical

biologist
massive
rumbling

Vocabulary Strategy for

Multiple-Meaning Words

Context Clues When you read, you may find that the meaning of a word you know does not make sense in a sentence. The word may have multiple meanings. You can look for clues to decide which meaning the author is using.

1. Try the meaning you know to see if it makes sense in the sentence.

2. If it doesn't make sense, think of another meaning for the word. Does that meaning make sense?

3. If that meaning doesn't make sense either, reread the words and sentences around the word. Use the context to help you figure out a meaning for the unknown word.

4. Try that meaning in the sentence. Check that it makes sense in the sentence.

As you read "Paradise Island," look for words that can have more than one meaning. Use context clues to help you figure out which meaning is being used.

Words to Write Reread "Paradise Island." Imagine you are visiting Paradise Island. Write a letter to a friend describing what the place is like. Use words from the *Words to Know* list in your writing.

PARADISE ISLAND

Welcome to Paradise Island! To find out more about what you can do on our island, check out these exciting activities.

• Walk or run on the gorgeous white sand beaches that ring the whole island. They were voted the Best Beaches in the World last year by *Touring* magazine!

• Swim in the beautiful blue-green waters of our lagoon. Protected from the ocean by a reef, the lagoon is also perfect for canoeing and kayaking.

• Take a walk with our staff biologist. You can learn about the many strange and colorful birds and other animals that live on the island.

• Climb the bluff for wonderful views of the island and the ocean. We offer climbs for beginners and experts.

• Take a day trip to the volcano. You can ride or hike to the top and look down into the massive crater. It has always been quiet (except for a rumbling noise every once in a while).

Paradise Island is a tropical paradise. Come see it for yourself and have the best vacation of your life!

Your Turn!

 Need a Review?
For additional help with multiple-meaning words, see pages 160–163.

 Ready to Try It?
As you read other text, use what you've learned about multiple-meaning words to help you understand it.

TEKS

4.2.B.1 Use the context of the sentence to determine meaning of an unfamiliar word.

Envision It! | Words to Know

aquarium

dolphins

flexible

enchanted

glimpses

pulses

surface

READING STREET ONLINE
VOCABULARY ACTIVITIES
www.TexasReadingStreet.com

Vocabulary Strategy for

Multiple-Meaning Words

Context Clues When you read, you may find that the meaning of a word you know does not make sense in a sentence. This may be because the word has more than one meaning. Sometimes the definition of the multiple-meaning word will be given in a nearby sentence. But often you will have to use context to determine the correct meaning of a multiple-meaning word.

1. Examine the word and try the meaning you know. Does it make sense in the sentence?

2. If it does not make sense, is there a definition of the word nearby? You can use it to figure out the word.

3. Try the meaning in the sentence and see if it makes sense.

As you read "Dolphins," use context clues to figure out multiple-meaning words. There may be a definition of the multiple-meaning word in a nearby sentence. Or there may be an example of the word in the same sentence.

Words to Write Reread "Dolphins." Imagine that you have an aquarium. What would you put in it? Describe your aquarium in a paragraph. Use the *Words to Know* in your description.

Dolphins

Dolphins are animals that live in the sea. Unlike many sea animals, they are mammals, not fish.

Dolphins have long, smooth bodies and flippers instead of fins. When they swim, dolphins move their tails up and down instead of side to side as fish do. Dolphins must go to the surface of the water to breathe. A dolphin breathes through a hole on top of its head.

Dolphins send out pulses or vibrations of sound to find things. The sound bounces off an object and back to the dolphin. The dolphin uses the sound to tell where the object is.

If you go to an aquarium or a zoo, you will most likely see bottle-nosed dolphins. They look like they are smiling. These animals are friendly and smart. They can be trained to jump through hoops, throw balls through nets, and "walk" backward on the water using their flexible tails.

People have long been enchanted by dolphins. The ancient Greeks drew pictures of them on pottery and walls. For centuries sailors have believed that catching glimpses of dolphins following their ships would bring them good luck.

Your Turn!

 Need a Review? For more help with multiple-meaning words, see pages 160–163.

Ready to Try It? As you read other text, use what you've learned about multiple-meaning words to help you understand it.

Envision It! Words to Know

concentrating

parachute

underbrush

dedication
essential
method
steer
wind

Vocabulary Strategy for

🔊 Homographs

Dictionary/Glossary Homographs are words that are spelled the same but have different meanings and sometimes different pronunciations. For example, *dove* is a homograph. *Dove* (duv) means "a kind of bird." *Dove* (long /o/ sound) means "jumped headfirst into water."

1. When you read a homograph, read the words and sentences around it.

2. Is there an example or definition of the word in the context? Put that meaning into the sentence and see if it makes sense.

3. If the word still doesn't make sense, use a dictionary or glossary to find the meaning.

As you read "Remembering Firefighting Heroes," use a dictionary or glossary to figure out the meanings of *wind* and *steer*.

Words to Write Reread "Remembering Fire-fighting Heroes." Figure out the meanings of the homographs in the passage. Write what you think each word means. Use a dictionary or glossary to check your work.

Remembering
Firefighting Heroes

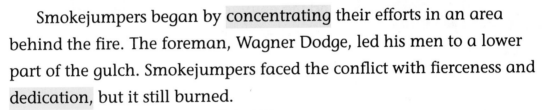

Smokejumpers are firefighters who parachute into remote areas and use the parachute to steer themselves near deadly fires. The U.S. Forest Service began using smokejumpers in 1940. They have become an essential part of protecting our country's national forests.

On August 5, 1949, a wildfire raged at Mann Gulch in Montana. A bolt of lightning had probably set fire to some underbrush near the Missouri River. At the same time, the wind picked up, feeding the fire even more.

Smokejumpers began by concentrating their efforts in an area behind the fire. The foreman, Wagner Dodge, led his men to a lower part of the gulch. Smokejumpers faced the conflict with fierceness and dedication, but it still burned.

Dodge realized that his method wasn't working. The fire was getting worse, so he ordered his men to run up the slope of the gulch to escape. At about the same time, the wind began blowing in the same direction, essentially chasing the firefighters up the hill. Fifteen men lost their lives.

In 1999, a dedication ceremony was held on the fiftieth anniversary of the fire. Smokejumpers landed in Mann Gulch to remember the sacrifice of those who had died.

Your Turn!

 Need a Review?
For additional help with homographs, see page 160.

▶ **Ready to Try It?**
As you read other text, use what you've learned about homographs to help you understand it.

TEKS

4.2.E.1 Use a dictionary or glossary to determine meanings of unknown words.

Vocabulary Strategy for

🔊 Multiple-Meaning Words

Envision It! Words to Know

dormitory

endurance

manual

boarding school

reservation

society

Dictionary/Glossary Sometimes you may read a word whose meaning you know, but that meaning doesn't make sense. The word may have more than one meaning. Use a dictionary or glossary to find the correct meaning.

1. Try the meaning that you know to see if it makes sense in the sentence.

2. If it doesn't, look up the word in a dictionary or glossary.

3. Find the entry for the word. The entries are in alphabetical order.

4. Read all the meanings given for the word. Try each meaning in the sentence.

5. Choose the meaning that makes the best sense in the sentence.

Read "Dreaming of Home." Use a dictionary or glossary to figure out the meanings of *reservation* and *manual* and other words with multiple meanings.

Words to Write Reread "Dreaming of Home." Imagine you went to school far away. Write about your feelings. Use words from the *Words to Know* list.

DREAMING OF HOME

Annie gazed out the window of the dormitory and longed to go outside. She knew that being outside would make her feel less homesick. But the students were required to do three hours of manual labor every day.

Annie's task was to wash the windows. While her hands were busy, her mind was back home on the reservation. There, she was talking to her mother and playing games with her sisters. Here, she lived in the dormitory with a hundred other girls. There, she was riding her pony and listening to her grandfather tell stories. Here, she sat in a classroom reciting English verbs.

Annie had not wanted to go away to boarding school, but that was the policy for Indian children in 1895. The school was supposed to teach them how to live in white society. Annie thought about what her father had said to her: "Akikta, remember the meaning of your name. You have determination. This experience will teach you patience and endurance."

Your Turn!

 Need a Review? For more help with multiple-meaning words, see pages 160–163.

Ready to Try It?
As you read other text, use what you've learned about multiple-meaning words to help you understand it.

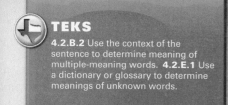

TEKS

4.2.B.2 Use the context of the sentence to determine meaning of multiple-meaning words. **4.2.E.1** Use a dictionary or glossary to determine meanings of unknown words.

Envision It! | Words to Know

capsule

horizon

module

astronauts

hatch

lunar

quarantine

READING STREET ONLINE
VOCABULARY ACTIVITIES
www.TexasReadingStreet.com

Vocabulary Strategy for

Multiple-Meaning Words

Context Clues Sometimes the meaning of a word you know does not make sense in a sentence. This is because the word has multiple meanings. Look for context clues to help you decide which meaning the author is using. If context clues don't help you, use a dictionary.

1. Try the meaning you know. Does it make sense in the sentence?

2. If that meaning doesn't make sense reread the words and sentences around the word. Use the context to help you find the meaning for the unknown word.

3. If it still doesn't make sense, look up the word in a dictionary and choose the meaning that makes sense in the sentence.

As you read "Travelers in Space," use context clues to figure out the meanings of *capsule* and *hatch* and other multiple-meaning words.

Words to Write Reread "Travelers in Space." Imagine you are traveling in space. Describe your spaceship and what you can see. Use words from the *Words to Know* list.

TRAVELERS in SPACE

Astronauts are space workers. Since the 1960s, they have blasted off into space. Astronauts explore the unknown, which is exciting. But much of their time is spent working hard.

They may repair a space station or a satellite. To do this, they suit up, open the hatch, and float out into space. When they finish the job, they float back into the spacecraft through a small door. Astronauts also do many experiments and make calculations related to their flight.

Early in the space program, there were many lunar flights. The astronauts took off in a huge spaceship. Part of it fell away after they got into orbit. Then they rode in a capsule, or small space vehicle. By the time they landed on the moon, the astronauts were riding in a module. This tiny spacecraft fit into the larger ship and could fly on its own.

The astronauts stood on the moon's surface and saw the Earth on the horizon! When they got back to Earth, they were in quarantine. They had to stay away from everyone to be sure they had not brought back any diseases.

Your Turn!

 Need a Review?
For additional help with multiple-meaning words, see pages 160–163.

 Ready to Try It?
As you read other text, use what you've learned about multiple-meaning words to help you understand it.

Base Words/Root Words

A base word, also called a root word, is a word that can't be broken into smaller words. *Friend* is a root of *friendly* and *friendship*.

Earth

Unearthly

Earth is the base word.

Strategy for Base Words

1. Look for a base word in the unknown word.
2. Determine the meaning of the base word.
3. Guess the meaning of the unfamiliar word. Does it make sense in the sentence?
4. Check the meaning in a dictionary.

178

Word Origins: Roots

Many English words contain Greek and Latin roots.

Dentures

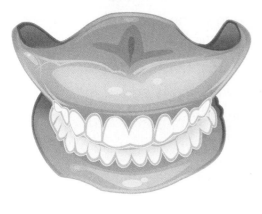

Telephone

Tractor

Latin Roots

dent	tooth
dict	to say; to speak
scrib	to write
sub	under; below
tract	to pull
vis	to see

Greek Roots

auto	self
bio	life
micro	very small
ology	the study of
phon	sound; voice
scope	see
tele	far

Strategy for Roots

1. Use what you know about Greek and Latin roots to guess the meaning of the unknown word.
2. Does your guess make sense in the sentence?
3. Use a dictionary to check your guess.

TEKS

4.2.A.6 Determine meaning of grade-level academic English words derived from other linguistic affixes.

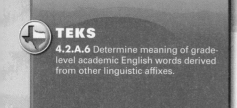

 Envision It! Words to Know

docks

migrating

scent

scan

wharf

yearned

**READING STREET ONLINE
VOCABULARY ACTIVITIES**
www.TexasReadingStreet.com

Vocabulary Strategy for

Affixes: Word Endings

Word Structure When you read an academic vocabulary word you don't know, you may be able to use the ending to figure out its meaning. Is -ed or -ing at the end of the word? The ending -ed is Old English and is added to a verb to make it past tense, or tell about past actions. The ending -ing is added to a verb to make it tell about present or ongoing actions.

1. Find a word that ends in -ed or -ing. Put your finger over the -ed or -ing.

2. Look at the base word. Do you know what the base word means?

3. Try your meaning in the sentence.

4. If it makes sense, add the ending and read the sentence again.

Read "Westward Ho!" Use what you know about endings to help you figure out this week's *Words to Know*.

Words to Write Reread "Westward Ho!" Imagine you are exploring an unknown river. Describe your first day on the water. Include details on what you see, hear, smell, and feel to help the reader experience your trip. Use words from the *Words to Know* list.

WESTWARD HO!

In the 1800s, America grew ever larger as land in the West was bought. As it grew, men and women of a certain kind yearned to travel west into the unknown. They had pioneer spirit.

There were no roads, of course. However, rivers made good highways for boats. In my mind I can see the pioneers with all their goods, waiting on the wharf in St. Louis. Sailors are busy loading and unloading ships. The pioneers load their belongings onto flatboats tied to the docks.

As they traveled, pioneers would scan the country for food and Indians. There were no grocery stores. And they never knew how the Indians would receive them. If the Indians were friendly, they might talk and trade. If a trapper was present, they were lucky. Trappers knew the country and the Indians well.

It must have been exciting to see this country for the first time. Pioneers saw endless herds and flocks of animals migrating. They breathed pure air full of the scent of tall grasses and wildflowers.

Your Turn!

 Need a Review?
For additional help with base words, see page 178.

 Ready to Try It?
As you read other text, use what you've learned about base words and word endings to help you understand it.

TEKS

4.2.A.3 Determine meaning of grade-level academic English words derived from other linguistic roots.

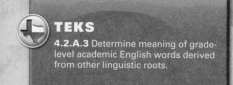

Envision It! | Words to Know

destruction

shatter

surge

expected

forecasts

inland

Vocabulary Strategy for

🎯 Root Words

Word Structure When you read an academic vocabulary word you do not know, try to identify the root word. The word *transport* has the Middle English root *port*, which means "to carry," and the prefix *trans-*, which means "across." Now you know the meaning of *transport* is "to carry across." Use what you know about root words as you follow these directions.

1. When you read an unknown word, first try to identify its root. The word *construction* contains the root word *construct*.

2. You may know that *construct* is "to build."

3. Look for a prefix, suffix, or ending in the word. The suffix *-ion* means "the act of" or "the result of." So *construction* means "the act of building."

4. Try the meaning in the sentence to see if it makes sense.

As you read "Hurricanes," use what you know about root words to figure out the meanings of academic words such as *destruction, moisture, tropical,* and other unknown words.

Words to Write Reread "Hurricanes." Have you ever been in a severe storm or seen one on TV? Write about the experience. Use words from the *Words to Know* list in your writing.

HURRICANES

A hurricane is a large storm with high winds and heavy rain. It needs heat and moisture to form, so the best hurricane-producing place is a tropical ocean. As warm, moist air rises, cooler air moves in. Then the air begins to spin. The winds spin around a calm center called the eye. The strongest winds are around the eye. They may have speeds of 200 miles per hour. A hurricane's winds may extend 250 miles from the eye.

If a hurricane stays over water, it keeps pulling heat and moisture from the ocean. But it begins to lose power as it reaches land, where the air is cooler and drier. Once it moves over land, it becomes weak very quickly.

The destruction from a hurricane comes from both wind and water. High winds shatter windows and uproot trees. Besides bringing heavy rain, a hurricane can cause a storm surge as winds push ocean water to areas far inland.

Meteorologists watch for and track hurricanes. They issue forecasts telling when a hurricane is expected to arrive so that people can prepare for the storm.

Your Turn!

 Need a Review?
For additional help with root words, see page 179.

 Ready to Try It?
As you read other text, use what you've learned about root words to help you understand it.

TEKS
4.2.A.1 Determine meaning of grade-level academic English words derived from Latin roots. 4.2.A.2 Determine meaning of grade-level academic English words derived from Greek roots.

scholars

temple

uncover

ancient
link
seeker
translate
triumph

Vocabulary Strategy for

Greek and Latin Roots

Word Structure Many words in English, especially academic vocabulary, have Greek and Latin roots. For example, the Latin *trans* in *translation* means "across, through, or beyond." The academic word *hieroglyphics* is made up of the Greek word parts *hieros,* meaning "holy," and *gluphe,* meaning "carving."

1. When you read an academic word you don't know, check the word for any Greek or Latin roots whose meanings you already know.

2. Use the meaning of the root to help you figure out the meaning of the unknown word.

3. Try the meaning in a sentence to see if it makes sense.

As you read "The Rosetta Stone," use Greek and Latin roots to help you figure out academic words, such as *scholars* and *archaeologists.*

Words to Write Reread "The Rosetta Stone." Imagine you've been asked by your school newspaper to interview Jean-François Champollion. Prepare a list of questions you will ask him about his life and his work on the Rosetta Stone. Use words from the *Words to Know* list as you write your questions.

The Rosetta Stone

In 1799, a French army officer found a stone slab near the city of Rosetta in Egypt. On the stone was the same announcement in three different languages. At the top was hieroglyphics, a writing that uses pictures or symbols to stand for ideas and sounds. This writing was used in ancient Egypt. In the middle was an Egyptian language called demotic. At the bottom was the Greek language.

For more than three thousand years, the ancient Egyptians used hieroglyphics on their temple walls and monuments. But over time the language was forgotten. For hundreds of years, scholars were unable to figure out how to read hieroglyphics.

Jean-François Champollion was a French scholar who wanted to be the first to read hieroglyphics. He studied the language his whole life. He was a true seeker of knowledge. He used the Greek part of the Rosetta Stone to translate the Egyptian part. The Rosetta Stone gave him a link between the known and the unknown.

Champollion's work was a triumph. It allowed other scholars and archaeologists to uncover the history of ancient Egypt.

Your Turn!

 Need a Review?
For additional help with Greek and Latin roots, see page 179.

 Ready to Try It?
As you read other text, use what you've learned about Greek and Latin roots to help you understand it.

TEKS

4.2.A.1 Determine meaning of grade-level academic English words derived from Latin roots. **4.2.A.2** Determine meaning of grade-level academic English words derived from Greek roots.

Envision It! | Words to Know

ruins

terraced

thickets

curiosity

glorious

granite

torrent

Vocabulary Strategy for

Greek and Latin Roots

Word Structure Many words, particularly academic vocabulary words, have Latin or Greek roots. The Latin root *terra* means "earth" or "land." It appears in *terrain* (surface of the ground) and *territory* (an area of land). The Greek root *graphikos* means "of writing" and *arkhaiologia* means "the study of ancient things." Knowing Latin and Greek roots can help you figure out unknown words.

1. Look at the unknown word. Try to identify a Greek or Latin root that you know.

2. Does the meaning of the Greek or Latin root give you a clue to the unknown word?

3. Try the meaning in the sentence to be sure it makes sense.

As you read "Looking for the Past," use what you know about Greek and Latin roots to help you figure out the meanings of *archaeologists, terraced,* and *graphics.*

Words to Write Reread "Looking for the Past." Imagine that you are a scientist looking for the past in a faraway land. Write a journal entry describing the sights you see and discoveries you make. Use words from the *Words to Know* list in your journal.

Looking for the Past

Some scientists called archaeologists study the past. They look at objects and buildings from past civilizations. They have curiosity about people who lived long ago. How did they live? What did they eat? What did they do every day? Did they read and write? Thanks to these scientists, we have learned a great deal about people who lived long ago.

These scientists have ventured into places that few others would go. They have cut their way through jungles with thickets full of dangerous animals. They have climbed steep mountains. They have crossed mountain rivers that fall in a raging torrent. They have found ruins of places people built long ago. These may look like nothing more than rocks to us, but they are glorious to these scientists.

Imagine a team of scientists as they discover terraced fields on the side of a mountain. These show that people long ago were clever farmers. Think of the scientists as they look at beautiful temples made of granite or marble. These show that people long ago had beliefs. Watch as the scientists carefully uncover clay pots decorated with unknown graphics. These show that people long ago were artistic and loved beauty.

Your Turn!

 Need a Review?
For additional help with Greek and Latin roots, see page 179.

▶ **Ready to Try It?**
As you read other text, use what you've learned about Greek and Latin roots to help you understand it.

TEKS

4.2.A.3 Determine meaning of grade-level academic English words derived from other linguistic roots. **4.2.A.6** Determine meaning of grade-level academic English words derived from other linguistic affixes.

Envision It! | Words to Know

generations

pulpit

shielding

avoided

ancestors

minister

numerous

READING STREET ONLINE
VOCABULARY ACTIVITIES
www.TexasReadingStreet.com

Vocabulary Strategy for

🎯 Root Words

Word Structure A root word is a word that other words are made from. The academic word *numerous* contains the Middle English root *numerus*, which means "number." If you know the root of a word, it can help you figure out the word's meaning.

1. Look at the word *avoided*. Does it have a root word you know?

2. How does the meaning of the prefix, suffix, or ending affect the meaning of the root?

3. Put together the root and the meaning of the prefix, suffix, or ending. The root word *avoid* means "to keep away from," and the ending *-ed* indicates past tense. *Avoided* means "to have kept away from."

4. Check to see that the meaning makes sense in the sentence.

As you read "Out of Slavery," use what you know about root words to figure out the academic words *courageous* and *nourishment*, and the *Words to Know*.

Words to Write Reread "Out of Slavery." Think about one of your ancestors. Write about what makes you proud of your ancestor. Use words from *Words to Know* in your article.

OUT OF SLAVERY

Slavery caused great hardship and sorrow in the United States. Africans were forced to come here as slaves. For generations slaves lived without freedom, and many white masters were cruel to them. All along, some white people said it was wrong to keep slaves. Over the years, more and more believed and said this. Often these voices came from the pulpit. It took a courageous minister to speak out and work for change. The number of people who wanted to free all slaves slowly grew.

Some very brave white and free black people helped slaves escape to freedom. They found numerous ways of shielding the runaway slaves. For example, helpers hid them in safe houses and gave them nourishment and clothes. Slaves who had run away avoided being seen by staying off roads and traveling at night.

Many people helped slaves to escape, but it took a long, terrible war to bring an end to slavery. Today African Americans remember their ancestors and are proud and thankful for the sacrifices they made.

Your Turn!

 Need a Review?
For additional help with root words, see pages 178–179.

 Ready to Try it?
As you read other text, use what you've learned about root words to help you understand it.

Genre

Literature is classified into different types, or **genres.**

- All genres are considered either fiction or nonfiction.
- Texts with similar form and style often belong to the same genre.
- Knowing the genre of a reading selection can help you better understand what you read.
- Knowing about genres can help you better choose what to read when you read independently.

Ready to Try It?

Envision It! | Genre

Fiction
fable
historical fiction
myth
realistic fiction
science fiction
tall tale
trickster tale

Drama

Poetry

Informational Text
expository text
persuasive text
procedural text

Literary Nonfiction
autobiography
biography
journal
personal essay

Fiction Describes imaginary events or people

	Genre	Settings	Characters	Plot
	A **fable** is a short, imaginative story that has a lesson, or moral.	Any; place and time may be unimportant to the story.	Animals are often the main characters.	Usually brief; moral usually stated at the end
	Historical fiction is a made-up story that takes place in the past.	Should be real or seem real; has specific focus on time and place in history	Like real people or based on real people; characters fit in with the historical time and place.	Any; conflict often about a struggle in the world at that time, or a great accomplishment
	A **myth** is an old story originally handed down by word of mouth. It may explain human behavior or events in nature.	Usually set in a fictional past, and often begins with "Long ago ..." or "There once was ..."	Animal characters can talk, think, and act like people.	Any; conflict is often between characters and nature, or between two characters.
	Realistic fiction is a made-up story that could really happen. It can include mysteries and adventure stories.	Should be real or seem real; may be specific to time	Think and act like real people	Realistic and believable
	Science fiction is a type of fantasy that tells a story based on science or technology.	Time and place is usually imagined; often set in the future	Characters may be realistic.	Any; conflict is often between characters and nature or technology, or between two characters.

	Genre	Setting	Characters	Plot
	A **tall tale** is an exaggerated story with characters that have superhuman abilities.	Often takes place in the past, sometimes in real places	Superhuman abilities; sometimes fictional versions of people in history	Any; story may also explain why or how something exists as it does today.
	A **trickster tale** is one type of folk tale that tells a story, or legend, about clever animals that outsmart or trick bigger and stronger animals or people.	Any; may be set in another time or place	Imaginary qualities; animals may do things that only people can do in real life.	Conflict is usually about the trickster wanting something from another character.

Drama and Poetry Tells a real or fictional story in a unique way

	Genre	Features	Organization	Includes...
	Drama tells a story that is meant to be performed.	Character dialogue and stage directions tell the story; information on characters and setting is included.	Lines of dialogue and stage directions	Plays; sketches; skits; scripts for radio or television
	Poetry is made up of words arranged in lines that have rhythm and may rhyme.	Lines of text that are rhythmic (have a beat); words that describe; poetic elements	Any; often in groups of lines called stanzas that use line breaks, rhyme, and meter	Limericks; free verse poems; humorous poems; lyrical poems; narrative poems; rhyming poems; sonnets; shape poems; ballads

Envision It! Genre

Informational Text Provides facts, details, and explanations

Genre	Features	Organization	Includes...
Expository text gives facts and details about people, places, things or events.	Facts and details about real places or events; usually includes maps, fact boxes, headings, time lines, or illustrations with captions	Can be chronological; may build from simple to more challenging information	Cause-and-effect, compare-and-contrast, problem-solution essays; magazine articles; articles about history or culture; historical documents
Persuasive text tries to convince readers to think or do something.	Tells the author's point of view; may use photos, illustrations, and persuasive words such as *must* and *should*	Often written with a cause-and-effect or problem-solution pattern; shows the writer's reasoning in a logical order	Editorials; letters to the editor; advertisements; some speeches; book, movie, or product reviews
Procedural text explains how to do something in clear, easy-to-understand steps.	Includes a list of materials (if needed); may use diagrams, charts, graphs, or illustrations	Usually chronological; may be numbered in order of steps	How-to texts; multi-step directions or instructions such as recipes or rules for a game

Literary Nonfiction Based on facts, real events, and real people

	Genre	Setting	Characters	Plot
	An **autobiography** is the story of a real person's life, written by that person.	A real place in the past, from the writer's life	Real people from real life	Any; conflict often about a great struggle, or an accomplishment
	A **biography** is the story of a real person's life, written by another person.	A real place in the past, from the subject's life	Real people from real life	Any; conflict often about a great struggle or accomplishment
	A **journal** is a record of a writer's thoughts and experiences.	May be abstract; usually current time and place of writer's life	Real people from real life	Any; entries usually focused on events from the writer's life and are not always connected. (Note: Fictional characters can keep journals too!)
	A **personal essay** is an account of an experience from the writer's life.	Any	Any; from real life	Any; story may focus on entertaining or informing readers about a topic.

My TEKS Chart

Using and Understanding Comprehension Strategies

☑ **Background Knowledge** I will make connections between literary and informational texts with similar ideas and support my ideas with details from the texts. **TEKS RC-4.F**

☑ **Important Ideas** I will summarize the main idea of a text and the details that support the main idea. **TEKS 4.11.A**

☑ **Inferring** I will make inferences about a text and use evidence from the text to support my understanding. **TEKS RC-4.D**

☑ **Monitor and Clarify** I will monitor my comprehension as I read and adjust my reading based on how well I understand the text. **TEKS RC-4.C**

☑ **Predict and Set Purpose** I will set a purpose for reading a text based on what I hope to get from the text or what others hope I will understand. **TEKS RC-4.A**

☑ **Questioning** I will ask different types of questions about a text. **TEKS RC-4.B**

☑ **Story Structure** I will tell the order of events in a story, summarize the events, and explain how they will influence future events in the story. **TEKS 4.6.A**

☑ **Summarize** I will summarize information in a selection, making sure the meaning and order are clear. **TEKS RC-4.E**

☑ **Text Structure** I will describe how the ideas are related in a text that is organized by causes and effects, sequence, or comparison. **TEKS 4.11.C**

☑ **Visualize** I will analyze how an author uses similes and metaphors to create imagery. **TEKS 4.8**

★ indicates review of previous TEKS or preparation for upcoming TEKS

Using and Understanding Comprehension Skills

☑ **Author's Purpose** I will explain the difference between an expository text in which an author directly states the purpose for writing and one in which the author does not directly state the purpose. **TEKS 4.10**

☑ **Cause and Effect** I will describe how the ideas are related in a text that is organized by causes and effects, sequence, or comparison. **TEKS 4.11.C**

☑ **Compare and Contrast** I will find similarities and differences between characters' experiences in a fictional story and the real-life experiences of the story's author. **TEKS 4.7**

☑ **Draw Conclusions** I will make inferences about a text and use evidence from the text to support my understanding. **TEKS RC-4.D**

☑ **Fact and Opinion** I will know the difference between a fact and an opinion in a text, and I will be able to tell why a fact is true. **TEKS 4.11.B**

☑ **Generalize** I will make a general statement about a text after given ideas about several things or people. ★

☑ **Graphic Sources** I will explain information shown in graphics. **TEKS 4.13.B**

☑ **Literary Elements** I will summarize and explain the theme—the lesson or message—of a piece of fiction. **TEKS 4.3.A** I will describe how the characters interact with one another and tell about the changes they undergo **TEKS 4.6.B**

☑ **Main Idea and Details** I will summarize the main idea of a text and the details that support the main idea. **TEKS 4.11.A**

☑ **Sequence** I will figure out the sequence of steps needed to do something. **TEKS 4.13.A**

★ indicates review of previous TEKS or preparation for upcoming TEKS

My TEKS Chart

Using and Understanding Vocabulary

☑ **Related Words** I will use context clues to figure out the meanings of words I don't know. **TEKS 4.2.B**

☑ **Context Clues** I will use context clues to figure out the meanings of words I don't know. **TEKS 4.2.B**

☑ **Antonyms and Synonyms** I will complete analogies based on what I know about synonyms and antonyms. **TEKS 4.2.C**

☑ **Prefixes and Suffixes** I will figure out the meanings of English words that have affixes. **TEKS 4.2.A**

☑ **Dictionary and Thesaurus** I will use a dictionary or glossary to find the meanings of words I don't know, figure out how to pronounce them, and learn how to divide them into syllables. **TEKS 4.2.E**

☑ **Multiple-Meaning Words** I will use context clues to figure out which meaning of a multiple-meaning word is being used. **TEKS 4.2.B**

☑ **Word Origins** I will figure out the meanings of English words that come from Latin, Greek, and other languages. **TEKS 4.2.A**

★ indicates review of previous TEKS or preparation for upcoming TEKS

Using and Understanding Genre

☑ **Fiction** I will summarize and explain the theme—the lesson or message—of a piece of fiction. TEKS 4.3.A I will compare and contrast the actions of characters in traditional and classic literature. TEKS 4.3.B

☑ **Drama** I will describe the characteristics of drama. TEKS 4.5

☑ **Poetry** I will explain how a poem's structure influences its form. TEKS 4.4

☑ **Informational Text** I will analyze, make inferences, and draw conclusions about expository text. TEKS 4.11

☑ **Literary Nonfiction** I will find similarities and differences between characters' experiences in a fictional story and the real-life experiences of the story's author. TEKS 4.7

★ indicates review of previous TEKS or preparation for upcoming TEKS

Acknowledgments

Text

The *Texas Essential Knowledge and Skills for English Language Arts and Reading* reproduced by permission, Texas Education Agency, 1701 N. Congress Avenue, Austin, TX 78701

Illustrations

78 Bill McGuire

Photographs

Every effort has been made to secure permission and provide appropriate credit for photographic material. The publisher deeply regrets any omission and pledges to correct errors called to its attention in subsequent editions.

Unless otherwise acknowledged, all photographs are the property of Pearson Education, Inc.

Photo locators denoted as follows: Top (T), Center (C), Bottom (B), Left (L), Right (R), Background (Bkgd)

46 (T) ©DK Images, (B) ©Lyn Balzer and Tony Perkins/Getty Images

57 (T) ©Gabriel Bouys/AFP/Getty Images, (B) ©Jamie & Judy Wild/Danita Delimont/Danita Delimont, Agent

63 Marital Colomb/Photodisc/Getty Images

65 ©Tom Brakefield/Corbis

73 Burstein Collection/Corbis

75 George E. Marsh Album/NOAA

91 ©Bettmann/Corbis

101 (T) ©Hisham Ibrahim/Corbis, (C) Daniel Thierry/Photononstop/PhotoLibrary Group, Ltd., (B) Tony Howell/PhotoLibrary Group, Ltd.

118 (T) Tetra Images/Getty Images

120 (C) ©Bill Stevenson/PhotoLibrary Group, Ltd., (T) ©david sanger photography/Alamy Images, (B) ©Goodshoot/Photolibrary

122 (T) ©Robert W. Ginn/Alamy Images, (B) Corbis/Jupiter Images, (C) Image100/Jupiter Images

124 (T) ©Oote Boe Photography/Alamy Images, (B) ©ScotStock/Alamy Images, (C) ©Thom Lang/Corbis

125 ©Bananastock /Jupiter Images

128 (T) Horizon International Images Limited/Alamy Images, (B) INTERFOTO Pressebildagentur/Alamy Images, (C) Robert Destefano/Alamy Images

130 (C) ©fStop/Alamy, (T) ©Heinrich van den Berg/Getty Images, (B,) Jupiter Images

132 (C) ©Juniors Bildarchiv/Alamy, (T) ©Phil Degginger/Alamy Images, (B) ©Westend61/Alamy

134 (T) ©Kari Marttila/Alamy Images, (C) ©Michael Coyne/Getty Images, (B) ©Nigel Cattlin/Alamy Images

138 (B) Flint/Corbis/Jupiter Images, (C) GoGo Images/Alamy, (T) Purestock/Photolibrary

140 (T) Images&Stories/Alamy Images, (C) Peter Barritt/Alamy Images, (B) Randy Faris/Jupiter Images

142 (B) David Madison/Getty Images, (C) Jupiter Images, (T) Lawrence Manning/Jupiter Images

143 (T) USDA Forest Service, Missoula, MT

144 (C) ©Richard Melloul/Sygma/Corbis, (T) John Lund/Getty Images, (B) Jupiter Images

145 ©Bettmann/Corbis

146 (B) Jenny Matthews/Alamy Images, (T) Richard Baker/Corbis, (C) Ron Niebrugge/Alamy Images

148 (C) ©Chad Ehlers/PhotoLibrary Group, Ltd., (T) ©Design Pics Eye Traveller/Photolibrary, (B) ©ImageState/Alamy Images

152 (B) Bill Miles/Corbis, (C) Grady Harrison/Alamy Images, (T) Paul Edmondson/Getty Images

154 (B) ©David Stoecklein/Corbis, (C) ©Paul A. Souders/Corbis, (T) ©Reuters/Corbis

156 (T) ©Danilo Calilung/Corbis, (C) AlaskaStock/PhotoLibrary Group, Ltd., (B) Image Source/Jupiter Images

158 (B) ©Enigma/Alamy, (T) ©Gray Mortimore/Getty Images, (C) ©Pat Doyle/Corbis

159 (T) ©Cindy Miller Hopkins/Danita Delimont/Alamy Images, (B) ©Sylvain Grandadam/Robert Harding Picture Library Ltd./Alamy

164 (B) Bilderbuch/Alamy, (C) Eyecandy Images/Index Open/Photolibrary, (T) Joe McDonald/Corbis